The March of War

The March of Wales, 1067–1300
A Borderland of Medieval Britain

MAX LIEBERMAN

UNIVERSITY OF WALES PRESS
CARDIFF
2008

Published by the University of Wales Press

University of Wales Press
10 Columbus Walk
Brigantine Place
Cardiff
CF10 4UP

www.uwp.co.uk

© Max Lieberman, 2008

The right of Max Lieberman to be identified as author of this work has been asserted by him in accordance with sections 77 and 78 of the Copyright, Designs and Patents Act 1988.

All rights reserved. No part of this book may be reproduced, stored in a retrieval system, or transmitted, in any form or by any means, electronic, mechanical, photocopying, recording or otherwise, without clearance from the publisher.

ISBN 978-0-7083-2116-4 (hb)
      978-0-7083-2115-7 (pb)

British Library Cataloguing-in-Publication Data.
A catalogue record for this book is available from the British Library.

Printed in Wales by Gwasg Dinefwr, Llandybïe

*For my parents, Dick and Marianne,
and for my brothers, David and Jesse*

Preface

This book is based on a series of six lectures I gave at the University of Oxford in 2005. In preparing those lectures and revising them for publication, I have incurred a number of debts of gratitude and I am very pleased to have the opportunity to acknowledge them.

I am deeply grateful to the late Professor Sir Rees Davies, who supervised my doctoral thesis, who suggested that I might write an introductory book on the March of Wales, and who generously gave me advice while I was planning my lectures.

I would like to thank Professor Thomas Charles-Edwards for introducing me to the medieval history of the British Isles, and for discussing my work with me on several occasions since then. I also offer my thanks to Professor Huw Pryce, who commented on a draft proposal for this book; to Dr John Reuben Davies, Professor John Gillingham, Dr Chris Lewis and Dr David Stephenson, who kindly sent me offprints and drafts of their work; to Vyv and Sylvia Lewis, who commented on the draft proposal for this book and helped with the proofreading; to the reader appointed by the University of Wales Press, for corrections and highly constructive comments and suggestions; and to Sarah Lewis, Elin Lewis and Siân Chapman at the University of Wales Press.

I am indebted to Dr Steven Gunn for proposing to the Faculty of History, Oxford, that I be given the status of Visiting Research Scholar for 2004–5; and to the Faculty for granting his request. Many thanks also, for being such excellent company, to my housemates of 2004–5, Dr Andrew Evans, Dr Carolina Moura-Alves, Dr Tracey Sowerby and Dr Tiffany Stern. Dr Moura-Alves came along to some of the lectures, and I am very grateful to her, and to the students who, fortunately, also attended, for questions and suggestions. Meanwhile, it has been a pleasure to write this book in the congenial surroundings of Wolfson College, Cambridge, and I thank the President and Fellows for electing me to be a Junior Research Fellow.

Collins Maps & Atlases kindly gave permission to publish the maps, which I created using Bartholomew mapping data.

Finally, I gratefully acknowledge the financial support I have received from the Swiss National Science Foundation.

This book is dedicated to my parents and my brothers. I hope it explains why I find the March of Wales so interesting.

Max Lieberman
Wolfson College, Cambridge

Contents

	Preface	vii
	List of Maps	xi
	Abbreviations	xii
1	Introduction	1
2	The Making of the March, 1066–1283	15
3	The Social and Economic March, 1067–1300	37
4	The Frontier of Peoples, 1067–1300	55
5	Kingdoms, Countries and Marches: the Context of the British Isles	75
6	Conclusion: the European Perspective	91
	List of Key Dates	105
	Bibliography	111
	Maps	127
	Index	139

Maps

1	The March of Wales in the fourteenth century	126
2	Wales and its borders in the eleventh century	127
3	The March in the making: the south-west	128
4	The March in the making: the south-east	129
5	The March in the making: the middle March	130
6	The March in the making: the north	131
7	Castles in Wales and the borders, 1066	132
8	Castles in Wales and the March, 1215	133
9	Castles in Wales and the March, 1300	134

Abbreviations

Arch. Camb.	*Archaeologia Cambrensis*
AWR	*The Acts of Welsh Rulers 1120–1283*, ed. H. Pryce (Cardiff, 2005)
BBCS	*Bulletin of the Board of Celtic Studies*
Brut	*Brut y tywysogyon*
Cartae	*Cartae et alia munimenta quae ad dominum de Glamorgancia pertinent*, ed. G. T. Clark, 2nd edn (6 vols, Cardiff, 1970)
DB	Domesday Book
EHD	*English Historical Documents*
GCH	T. B. Pugh (ed.) and G. Williams (gen. ed.), *Glamorgan County History*, vol. 3, *The Middle Ages* (Cardiff, 1971)
Mon. Ang.	*Monasticon Anglicanum*
ODNB	*Oxford Dictionary of National Biography* (Oxford, 2004)
PRS	Pipe Roll Society
RCAHMW	Royal Commission on the Ancient and Historical Monuments of Wales
PRO/TNA	The National Archives, formerly the Public Record Office, Kew
RS	Rolls Series
TRHS	*Transactions of the Royal Historical Society*
WHR	*Welsh History Review*

1

Introduction

Nowadays, the Welsh borders are often referred to as the 'March of Wales' or the 'Welsh marches'. This usage has a long tradition. The Welsh borders, or parts of them, were already identified as the 'March' in such documents as Domesday Book (1086) and Magna Carta (1215).[1] In medieval history, however, the expression 'the March of Wales' has a specific meaning. Historians use it to refer to a part of medieval Wales: the part which was gradually occupied by Norman and English knights between *c.*1067 and 1282–3, and which then remained separate from the Principality of Wales until the Acts of Union of 1536 and 1542.

The last Welsh war of Edward I, king of England, which took place in 1282–3, is a watershed in the history of the March of Wales. Over the two centuries leading up to that war, the extent of the March varied a good deal over time, as the Welsh lost ground to foreign occupiers and then gained it back again. But in the campaigns of 1282–3, Edward I succeeded in gaining direct control over the north and west of Wales, which had resisted conquest until then. The prince of Wales, Llywelyn ap Gruffudd, was killed during the war; his brother Dafydd was captured and executed. The military success of Edward I brought to an end the first, formative phase in the history of the March of Wales. After his occupation of native Wales in 1282–3, no further conquests of Welsh territory were possible.

In 1301, Edward I bestowed on his only surviving son, the future Edward II, the title of prince of Wales. But the land that came with the title, the so-called Principality of Wales, only comprised the north and west of the country: Anglesey, Snowdonia and Ceredigion. The rest of Wales was the March in its fully fledged state: a patchwork of conquest territories, about forty in all, of widely varying size and age. Ever since about a year after 1066, when the Normans who had defeated the English at Hastings arrived on the Welsh borders, the prospect of conquest had drawn military adventurers to Wales. Most of them had come from Normandy or from England, and many had been quite successful at staking out a claim. Invariably, they had proceeded by raiding a particular part of Wales and then fortifying it as best they could, by building castles and granting some of the land to the knights of their retinues. Many of the conquest territories which took shape in this way had been named after the ancient Welsh kingdoms and commotes which they had displaced: Brecon after Brycheiniog, Gower after Gŵyr, or Glamorgan after Morgannwg. Other Marcher lordships had taken the name of border castles: for instance, Clifford, Monmouth and Montgomery. Yet others, such as Denbigh and Dyffryn Clwyd, had recently been established by Edward I and granted to the captains of his Welsh campaigns.[2]

After 1282–3, the March of Wales could no longer be further expanded by military conquest. Nevertheless, even then, the final extent of the March had not yet quite been determined, for the March was also encroaching eastwards upon English territory. This was because Marcher lords, to all intents and purposes, thought of themselves as kings within their own lordships. For instance, they claimed the right to lead their knights to war against the Welsh whenever they wished, and to adjudicate on the most serious legal cases, which in England could only be brought before the king: arson or murder, say, the so-called pleas of the crown. Marcher lords not only tried such pleas themselves, if they arose in their lordships; they had their own gallows, that is, the right and means to inflict the penalty of death. Such outrageous claims to 'Marcher liberties' did not go uncontested, particularly in lordships which bordered on or even overlapped with English territory, and particularly after about 1200, by which time English royal officials had begun to venture more regularly into the border counties. Nevertheless, even after 1200, the Marcher lords seized every chance they got to withdraw English border territories into the March, that is, to prevent intrusions by the agents of the English kingdoms, be they sheriffs, justices of the peace or tax collectors. In one colourful case which occurred in 1250, Walter Clifford, lord of Clifford on the Welsh borders of Herefordshire, was stung in his Marcher pride by the peremptory style of a letter from Henry III, and forced the messenger to eat that letter along with the royal seal.[3] The medieval kingdom of England is rightly regarded as the most advanced 'state' of Europe, precocious in such areas as its development of parliament, the governance of localities from the centre, bureaucracy, taxation and law. Yet the tenacity and success of the Marcher lords in eluding its grasp meant that even the English kingdom did not quite achieve entirely clear-cut borders.

INTRODUCTION

Moreover, in 1301, the March was exceptionally fragmented and diverse. The 100-kilometre journey from Shrewsbury, say, westwards to the castle of Dolforwyn in the March and thence onwards to the Principality could have been made in two days by a rider on horseback.[4] Such a journey would have begun in an English county town with its royal castle and resident sheriff, monthly meetings of the shire court and regular visits from the royal tax collectors. On its way to Wales the journey would have continued through the valley of the Rea and the Camlad, which was guarded by Caus castle. In 1301, the land here belonged to the family of Corbet. The lord of the castle, Peter Corbet, was descended in male line from the Norman knight who had been granted this part of Shropshire by Roger de Montgomery, the first earl of Shrewsbury. Peter fancied himself a Marcher lord. He ran his lordship like a small kingdom: he had his own gaol and had recently been berated by royal officials for incarcerating and ransoming tenants.[5] He was fond of asserting that he and his ancestors had tried pleas of the crown at Caus since time immemorial, though in 1292 he had been told that Caus lay in the county 'where no one should be king except the king of England'.[6] From Caus, it would have been a short trip to Offa's Dyke, and beyond that lay the royal border lordship of Montgomery. Originally established by Roger, earl of Shrewsbury, in the late eleventh century, it had been held by the de Bollers family until 1207, when it escheated to the crown. Since then, it had been placed in the hands of a succession of royal stewards. Further west, up the Severn valley, lay Dolforwyn castle. Dolforwyn had first been built in 1273, by Llywelyn ap Gruffudd, the prince of Wales who was killed in 1282. In 1277, Dolforwyn had been captured by the English, and become the centre of the new Marcher lordship of Ceri, which Edward I had granted to Roger Mortimer of Wigmore, one of his ablest military commanders. From Dolforwyn, it was another forty kilometres or so across the Welsh mountains to Meirionydd, which in 1284 had been converted into a constituent shire of the Principality by the Statute of Rhuddlan. Today, this journey would pass from Shropshire through Montgomeryshire to Merionethshire. In 1301, it would have passed through five different kinds of territory: an English county (Shropshire); a lordship established on shire ground with aspirations to being a liberty (Caus); a former Marcher lordship which had escheated to the crown (Montgomery); a Welsh commote which had been converted into a Marcher lordship by Edward I (Ceri); and the former Welsh *cantref* of Meirionydd, then a constituent shire of the Principality. In the south of the country, there were considerably larger Marcher lordships. But these were actually subdivided into smaller units of aristocratic power centred on the castles of the lord's military tenants: in Glamorgan, such sublordships included Ogmore and Coity.

Such was the March of Wales in 1301. It was a region with a history quite unique within Britain. There were certainly no Marcher lordships on the Anglo-Scottish border. That border had only been finally settled on the Solway–Tweed line in 1157, when Henry II of England browbeat the young Malcolm IV of Scotland into surrendering Cumberland, Westmorland and Northumberland.[7] But even before that date, no Norman knight or baron had dared ride alone against the king of Scots with a view to carving out a piece of that king's territory. Fairly large and compact lordships in fact abounded on both sides of the Solway–Tweed line, throughout the twelfth and thirteenth centuries. But these had originated as grants conferred by the kings of England or of Scotland, not as local territorial conquests made by freelancing knights and barons.[8] In the south-west of Scotland, for instance, Normans, by 1165, held the lordships of Annandale and of Liddesdale.[9] In the north of England west of the Pennines, much of English Cumbria consisted of great tenurial blocks. Moreover, to the north of Carlisle castle, the barony of Liddel Strength bordered on Scotland, while that of Burgh by Sands looked across the Solway Firth to Galloway. East of the Pennines, baronies and castleries abounded, but apart from Wooler and Wark on Tweed, they lay at some distance to the south of the border, for instance at Alnwick, Prudhoe and Redesdale, Bywell, Mitford, and Morpeth.[10] Mostly they had originally been meant to guard the lowlands from brigands in the Pennines. As for the barony of Wark on Tweed, it tended to be held by the English crown during times of crisis; Roxburgh, Berwick and Norham were royal castles.

On the English side of the Scottish border, some of the lords did hold territories referred to by historians to as 'liberties'.[11] The king of Scotland himself held the 'liberty of Tynedale' which extended both into Northumberland and Cumberland. This, in 1234, was found to lie 'beyond the king of England's power'.[12] The lords of the English liberties, too, had singularly wide-ranging privileges, including a right to a gallows. But these privileges fell short of the quasi-regal immunity encountered in the March of Wales, since they excluded pleas of the crown.[13] In short, these were liberties, but they lay firmly within the English kingdom. A large part of the explanation for their origin was clearly that they only came fully into the ambit of the English 'state' after 1157.

INTRODUCTION

The medieval March of Wales was a unique part of the political geography of Britain. It was also remarkably long-lived. As mentioned, it gradually took shape between about 1067 and 1300. It existed for another two and a half centuries. In all, it remained largely outside the grasp of English royal government for well-nigh five hundred years. Indeed, the imposition of direct royal control spelled the end of the medieval March of Wales. With the Acts of Union of England and Wales of 1536 and 1542, Henry VIII and his Parliament converted the Marcher lordships into new Welsh shires, such as Pembrokeshire or Montgomeryshire, or incorporated them into the old English border counties (Cheshire, Shropshire, Herefordshire and Gloucestershire).

It is quite astounding that the March survived for so long. Before 1283, it was a source of constant irritation and provocation to the rulers of the Welsh kingdoms and principalities. Moreover, even though it lay on the periphery of the English kingdom, the March of Wales was often a thorn in the side of the kings of England. The Norman and Plantagenet kings of England were no strangers to the need to deal with unruly subjects. But the Marchers were in a league of their own. Even a single Marcher lord could cause a king no end of trouble. In the early 1230s, Richard Marshal, the earl of Pembroke, led a rebellion which was backed by his troops from Wales and Ireland as well as several other Marcher lords, aggravating Henry III to the point where the king swore he would not have peace with the earl unless he came before him with a rope around his neck to beg for forgiveness.[14]

Even the smaller fry among the Marcher lords were a force to be reckoned with. By the fourteenth century, and probably much earlier, the larger Marcher lordships like Pembroke or Glamorgan contained around fifty or sixty knights' fees. Most, like Brecon, Caus, Clun or Gower, contained around twenty to thirty. This may not have been much compared to some of the great earldoms of England. But unlike the holders of English knights' fees, the knights in the March almost all owed their service not to the king of England, but to their Marcher lords. This meant that the Marchers had considerable military clout to back up their spirit of independence. Because of their unique position, even a few of them could exert great influence on the course of events during the crises of the English kingdom (such as in 1215–16 or 1263–5). Moreover, some of the most formidable of the English magnates numbered among them. For much of the twelfth century, and then again from the thirteenth, the earls of Gloucester were also lords of Glamorgan. The Bohuns, earls of Hereford, of Essex and of Northampton, were at the height of their power in the thirteenth and fourteenth centuries, when they were also in control of the lordships of Brecon and sometimes of Builth and of Haverford. From the thirteenth century on, the lords of Oswestry and of Clun on the Welsh borders of Shropshire were also earls of Arundel.

The Marchers' influence on later medieval British history was grimly foreshadowed during the reign of Edward II, the first English king to have been prince of Wales. The woes of Edward II's reign grew a good deal worse when he insisted on helping his favourites, the Despensers, amass great landed wealth in the March. The opposition to him was led by Roger Mortimer, the first earl of March, a descendant of one of the oldest Marcher families. Mortimer became the lover of Edward II's queen, Isabella, and orchestrated the king's deposal and gruesome murder in 1327, before being publicly executed himself as a traitor. The second earl of Arundel, Edmund Fitzalan, himself a Marcher lord, was beheaded in 1326, allegedly on Mortimer's orders. Nevertheless, the March survived for centuries longer, even after the rebellion of Owain Glyn Dŵr, which began in September 1400 and raged for a decade and a half, partly because the Marcher lords refused to obey royal commands to cooperate in quelling it. It is ironic to note that the Tudors were able to succeed to the throne of England at the end of the fifteenth century partly because of their great landed base in the March of Wales.

Fortunately for the kings of England, the Marchers never united in a cause against them. Lords of the March were to be found in both camps in the civil war of Stephen's reign (1135–53) and in the great thirteenth-century crises under John and Henry III. It is also true that the Marchers remained subjects of the English kings. When a Marcher lord died leaving a minor heir, or indeed no heir, his Marcher castles and lands passed temporarily into royal custody, just like lands in England. Walter Clifford, we are told, received the death penalty for the outrageous cheek with which he had treated a king's messenger; he was pardoned, but Henry III had made his point.[15] Edward I scored some famous victories over some of the most powerful Marcher lords; in the early 1290s, the lords of Glamorgan (the earl of Gloucester and Hertford) and of Brecon (the earl of Hereford) were forced to acknowledge that the king of England should pass judgment in their boundary dispute. Indeed, at a parliamentary session at Westminster in 1292, those two earls were condemned to prison, and their Marcher possessions confiscated.[16]

The Marchers were always a problem for the king of England. Yet, in other respects the two phases in the history of the March contrast starkly with each other. Perhaps the most striking difference is that the first period was almost exclusively the formative one. The March took shape in the two hundred-odd years between 1066 and 1283, between the Norman conquest of England and the English conquest of Wales. This was its heroic age. After *c.*1300, it became fossilized, its only reasons for continued existence being the vested interests and the by then customary rights of the Marcher lords. From this follows the importance of the early period. A thorough grounding in the first two centuries of Marcher history is indispensable for a full understanding of their late medieval aftermath.

The creation of the March had momentous consequences not only for Wales but also for the wider history of medieval and early modern Britain. Marcher history offers a unique and complementary perspective on British political history. But the March of Wales is also an intrinsically interesting region because it was one of the borderlands of medieval Britain. It was a borderland in political and administrative terms. It was also a region where different societies met and intermingled. Discovering the origins of the March obviously bears on Welsh and English political history. The March was one of Britain's chief power bases for aristocratic rebels. But it is also of interest to social and cultural historians. This is because much can be learned about societies by looking at their margins, and about countries by looking at their frontiers.

Writing a book about a subject implies that that subject is a separate and self-contained topic. That needs some justification in the case of the March of Wales. On the one hand, it might be proposed that the history of the March is a part of Welsh history, and should be told as such. On the other hand, it might be questioned whether there is a single history of the March at all, or whether on closer inspection it disintegrates into the trials and tribulations of the individual Marcher lordships. One might respond to the first point that some of the 'Marcher' lordships lay wholly or partly on English territory. To the second point, it might be retorted that contemporaries clearly thought of the March as one region. This book will argue that there is much to be gained from studying the March as a subject in its own right.

This book is about what the future of Marcher studies might look like. It will, therefore, be fruitful to discuss briefly what their past has been. The roots of Marcher studies go deep. The medieval Marcher lords themselves were keenly interested in the deeds of their ancestors and the origins of their lordships. By the late thirteenth century, the Fitzwarins of Whittington were being entertained by partly fantastical tales about their forebears, most of whom were called Fulk. These tales told of the first Fulk Fitzwarin, who came into possession of Whittington castle; and of the outlawry during John's reign of Fulk Fitzwarin III.[17] We also have the more sober family chronicle of the Mortimers of Wigmore, penned in Latin in the fourteenth century.[18] Common to both texts – and to other similar ancestral legends from the March – is what has been called the 'Marcher ethos'. The belief that the lords of the March were descended from the doughty knights who had been guarding the Welsh borders since the days of William the Conqueror was an exceedingly popular one in late medieval times. Ralph Mortimer, we are told, after 'fighting like a lion' on the field of Hastings in 1066, was sent 'as a fierce champion to the March'.[19] The romance of *Fouke le Fitz Waryn* sets its scene with a passage describing William the Conqueror's first appearance on the Welsh borders: 'the king thought he would give all the lands of the March to the bravest knights in all his host so that they might defend the March against [the Welsh] for their benefit and for the honour of their lord the king'.[20]

Both stories may in fact have been equally far-fetched (there is no corroborating evidence that Ralph Mortimer fought at Hastings), but one can easily see why they would have appealed to medieval Marcher lords. Indeed, the claim that the Marchers were hand-picked by the Conqueror and put in charge of the Welsh border was confidently put forward for many years, and endured beyond the end of the March of Wales in 1536–42. For it was a short step from this idea to claiming that the Marcher liberties derived from a royal grant arising from services rendered in the defence of the English kingdom against the Welsh. That step was taken with gusto in the sixteenth century, by George Owen of Henllys, a lawyer and antiquary who acquired the lordship of Cemais in northern Pembrokeshire and became deeply interested in the origins of the Marcher lordships.[21]

This view held sway until well into the twentieth century. The appearance, in 1911, of J. E. Lloyd's two-volume work, *A History of Wales from the Earliest Times to the Edwardian Conquest*, has been said to 'inaugurate Welsh history as a modern academic subject'.[22] It is a great scholar's masterpiece and based on an unprecedented familiarity with the sources; its second volume provides an indispensable survey, in narrative form, of Welsh history from the coming of the Normans to 1283. But it well exemplifies how uneasily the history of the March sits with the history of *pura Wallia*, native Wales. The Normans and their lordships feature in Lloyd's work in much the same way as they do in the medieval Welsh chronicles themselves: as being alien to Wales and its history. It may be that Lloyd considered Marcher liberties to be a matter for the constitutional history of England; in any case, he does not discuss their origin or nature in his *History of Wales*.

The March and its liberties escaped close scrutiny until 1956. In that year, another great historian of Wales, Goronwy Edwards, voiced his deep-seated doubts that any royal grant of liberties ever took place. Noting that the Normans often laid claim to entire Welsh commotes, he argued that in doing so the conquerors usurped the rights which had been due the Welsh kings from those territorial units.[23] However, this argument itself is no longer universally accepted. Indeed, a leading Welsh historian of the following generation, Rees Davies, presented a view of the making of Marcher liberties which to date has remained unchallenged, and moreover has recently helped stimulate interest in the liberties and franchises which existed elsewhere in Britain.[24] He argued that 'constitutional' or legal niceties, whether English or Welsh, were the last thing the first Norman conquerors worried about.[25] Waging war against the Welsh was a fact of life for them, whether or not they had been granted the privilege to do so. The jurisdictional powers over their tenants developed from the conditions of closely knit colonial communities which needed to survive in a hostile environment. In Davies's view, the so-called Marcher liberties only came to be so identified in the thirteenth century, and particularly from 1240. At that time the kings of England enjoyed a spell of dominance over Wales and the March. Moreover, the English 'state', particularly its central administration, had developed to a point where it began to intrude more regularly in the peripheries of the English kingdom. In particular, it became closely interested in its own customary rights and privileges (and their financial value). This led it to challenge and question the entrenched rights and privileges of the competition, to wit, other aristocratic landholders. In the thirteenth century, the Marcher lords had to defend their legal right to practices their forebears had taken for granted, because they had begun to be interpreted in legal terms by the English government.[26]

Writing about the March is always a balancing act. Studies of individual Marcher lordships can devote more space to the development of individual lordships and the variety that existed even within them. Survey studies can concentrate on the comparative perspective and on the March as a whole, revealing its common characteristics and the diversity within the larger picture.[27] Much invaluable work has already been done, ranging across the spectrum from more localized to more general works. Attention should be drawn to the existing Welsh county histories (notably Glamorgan, Pembroke and Gwent); to articles in the journals of local historical societies and in *Archaeologia Cambrensis*, the *Transactions of the Honourable Society of Cymmrodorion*, the *Bulletin of the Board of Celtic Studies*, the *National Library of Wales Journal,* and *Welsh History Review*;[28] and to a number of unpublished doctoral theses.[29]

As for survey studies, these are particularly valuable in flagging up the 'international' context of the March, its place within the wider history of Britain, Ireland and indeed Europe. Michael Altschul's work on the Clare earls of Gloucester, though entitled *A Baronial Family in Medieval England*, was one of the first discussions whose remit extended both to England and the March.[30] A great debt is owed by Marcher historians to the work of Rees Davies, which includes the fullest general studies of the March as well as notable local contributions. His *Lordship and Society in the March of Wales, 1282–1400* (1978) ranges particularly widely and marshals a vast amount of documentary evidence.[31] Its many-faceted analysis of aristocratic power in the March places that phenomenon within its European context. That is to say, it draws out the affinities of lordship in the March with the concept and practice of aristocratic power in England as well as on the Continent. The analysis of lordship is complemented by a conspectus of Marcher society and economy. Its focus is on the fourteenth century, but the formative phase of the March is a recurring theme in this remarkable study as well. More recently, Rees Davies's volume in the Oxford History of Wales series provides a pellucid survey of the making of the March, of the definition of Marcher liberties, and of the region's later history.[32]

Thus, the March has already received considerable attention as a subject in its own right, albeit with a focus on the origins of the Marcher liberties and on the second, post-1283 phase in its history. But the March also bears very directly on a range of related fields of historical investigation. For one thing, it is not easy to bracket the history of the March exclusively with either Welsh or English history; it is tied to both. Because of this, it has strong links to a new trend in medieval historiography which seeks to overcome, and thereby to complement, a 'compartmentalized' approach to the national histories of England, Scotland, Wales and Ireland. The move towards thinking integrally about the British Isles was given a forceful impetus in 1956 by Geoffrey

Barrow's *Feudal Britain*; it has been gathering momentum ever since.[33] A central concern has been to compare and contrast the countries of the British Isles during the medieval period, and thereby to recognize more clearly the contours of a larger picture, for instance with regard to the political and cultural impact of the Normans and the English; the definition and survival of 'ethnic' identities; or the very shaping of countries.[34]

As a borderland, the March of Wales is even of interest to the wider world beyond the British Isles. Historical frontiers have long been scrutinized by scholars to glean information about the states and countries they delimited. They have also long been a topic of study in their own right. Several volumes of collected articles, as well as monographs, testify to this.[35] One task that historians have set themselves is to discover how political boundaries were demarcated and perceived. But an interest in political boundaries, in the frontiers of kingdoms and principalities, is also inextricably linked to the historical investigation of peoples.

The March, by virtue of being a borderland of medieval Britain, has much to offer historians. The following chapters aim to re-emphasize and update that point. They explore some of the ways in which the early history of the March is relevant to the issues nowadays on historians' minds. They aim to plot possible avenues for future research. Since they branch out in quite different directions thematically, a short survey will be helpful. The next chapter will sketch the contours of the political and military history of the March *c.*1067–1300. This chapter is supplemented by a list of key dates. Chapter 3 will argue that the economic and social history of the March is the concomitant of military conquest and domination. Studying frontiers invariably involves comparing and contrasting societies, and Chapter 4 will discuss what the March may tell us about ethnic identities in Britain, particularly those of the Welsh and the English. The March of Wales clearly also has much to tell us about what constituted a boundary between two countries, or between two different kinds of kingdoms, in the Middle Ages. Chapter 5 is therefore devoted to finding the place of the March in the medieval history of the creation of the countries of Britain. Chapter 6, finally, attempts to draw together the different themes by contending that the March was a borderland of Europe as well as of Britain. All chapters will argue that much remains to be discovered about the history of the March. This book attempts to draw attention to rather than to fill some of the gaps in our knowledge. It will have amply served its purpose if it helps to foster interest in the borderlands of medieval Britain.

Notes

1. DB 183 ('in marcha de Wales'), 186 ('in Marcha de Walis'); J. C. Holt, *Magna Carta*, 2nd edn (Cambridge, 1992), app. 6, esp. pp. 467–9 (clause 56 of the 1215 text). Like Domesday's Latin term, the English word 'march', in the sense of 'borderland', derives from the Germanic roots that also gave rise, for instance, to the name 'Denmark'.
2. The Principality was assigned as a patrimony to English kings' heirs apparent for the rest of the Middle Ages, and indeed until 1727. Since then, the title of prince of Wales has been bestowed without ownership of the crown estates in Wales. Cf. J. G. Edwards, *The Principality of Wales, 1267–1967: A Study in Constitutional History* (Denbigh, 1969), esp. app. D.
3. Matthew Paris, *Chronica majora*, ed. H. R. Luard (7 vols, RS, 1872–83), v, 95.
4. On the speed of medieval travellers in England cf. F. M. Stenton, 'The road system of medieval England', *Economic History Review*, 7 (1936), 1–21.
5. *Select Bills in Eyre, 1292–1333*, ed. W. C. Bolland (Selden Society, 30, 1914), pp. 37–8: cf. M. Lieberman, 'Striving for Marcher liberties: the Corbets of Caus in the thirteenth century', in M. Prestwich (ed.), *Liberties and Identities in Later Medieval Britain* (Woodbridge, forthcoming).
6. *Placita de quo warranto*, ed. W. Illingworth (London, 1818), p. 686a.
7. In the Treaty of York of 1237, Alexander III of Scotland surrendered his claim to Cumberland, Westmorland and Northumberland, while Henry III of England conceded to him the honour of Tynedale as well as Cumbrian lands around Penrith. Cf. *EHD*, i, no. 31, pp. 354–5.
8. I. J. Sanders, *English Baronies: A Study of their Origin and Descent, 1086–1327* (Oxford, 1960); G. W. S. Barrow, *The Anglo-Norman Era in Scottish History* (Oxford, 1980).
9. P. G. B. McNeill, H. L. MacQueen and A. M. Lyons (eds), *Atlas of Scottish History to 1707* (Edinburgh, 1996), pp. 412–13; G. W. S. Barrow, 'The pattern of lordship and feudal settlement in Cumbria', *Journal of Medieval History*, 1 (1975), 130–2.
10. Sanders, *Baronies*. Cf. maps in Barrow, 'Cumbria', 121–4; and in W. E. Kapelle, *The Norman Conquest of the North: The Region and its Transformation, 1000–1135* (London, 1979), p. 143.
11. J. C. Holt, *The Northerners: A Study in the Reign of King John* (Oxford, 1961); cf. M. Prestwich (ed.), *Liberties and Identities* (Woodbridge, forthcoming).
12. *Curia Regis Rolls*, vol. 15, *1233–37* (London, 1972), nos. 960, 1259.
13. Holt, *Northerners*, pp. 197–9.
14. Matthew Paris, *Chron. maj.*, ii, 265.
15. Ibid., v, 95.
16. *The Parliament Rolls of Medieval England, 1275–1504*, gen. ed. C. Given-Wilson (16 vols, London, 2005), vol. 1, *1275–94*, ed. P. Brand (London, 2005), 499–516.
17. *Fouke le Fitz Waryn*, ed. E. Hathaway, P. T. Ricketts, C. A. Robson and A. D. Wilshere (Oxford, 1975).

INTRODUCTION

[18] *Mon. Ang.*, vi, 348–56.
[19] Ibid., p. 348.
[20] *Fouke*, ed. Hathaway et al., p. 3, ll. 23–6.
[21] George Owen of Henllys, *The Description of Pembrokeshire*, ed. D. Miles (Llandysul, 1994), esp. ch. 3.
[22] J. E. Lloyd, *A History of Wales from the Earliest Times to the Edwardian Conquest* (London, 1911; 3rd edn 1939); cf. R. R. Davies, 'Lloyd, Sir John Edward, 1861–1947', *ODNB*.
[23] J. G. Edwards, 'The Normans and the Welsh March', *Proceedings of the British Academy*, 42 (1957 for 1956), 155–77; the view is echoed by B. G. Charles, *George Owen of Henllys: A Welsh Elizabethan* (Aberystwyth, 1973), p. 132.
[24] Cf. Prestwich (ed.), *Liberties and Identities*.
[25] R. R. Davies, 'Kings, lords and liberties in the March of Wales, 1066–1272', *TRHS*, 5th ser., 29 (1979), 41–61.
[26] Cf. also H. M. Cam, 'The evolution of the mediaeval English franchise', *Speculum*, 32 (1957), 427–42; repr. in eadem, *Law-Makers and Law-Finders* (London, 1962), pp. 22–43.
[27] L. H. Nelson, *The Normans in South Wales, 1070–1171* (Austin, TX, and London, 1966); D. Walker, *The Norman Conquerors* (Swansea, 1977); A. C. Reeves, *The Marcher Lords* (Swansea, 1983); M. Lieberman, *The Medieval Concept of the March of Wales* (Cambridge, forthcoming).
[28] T. B. Pugh (ed.) and G. Williams (gen. ed.), *Glamorgan County History*, vol. 3, *The Middle Ages* (Cardiff, 1971); R. F. Walker (ed.), *Pembrokeshire County History*, vol. 2, *Medieval Pembrokeshire* (Haverfordwest, 2002); R. A. Griffiths, T. Hopkins and R. Howell (eds), *The Gwent County History, vol. 2, The Age of the Marcher Lords, c.1070–1536* (Cardiff, 2006). The following volumes for Gwent and for Ceredigion take the story from prehistory to the coming of the Normans: M. J. Aldhouse-Green and R. C. Howell (eds), *The Gwent County History*, vol. 1, *Gwent in Prehistory and Early History* (Cardiff, 2004); J. L. Davies and D. P. Kirby (eds), *Cardiganshire County History*, vol. 1, *From the Earliest Times to the Coming of the Normans* (Cardiff, 1994, repr 2001); cf. also J. G. Jones and E. M. White (eds), *Cardiganshire County History*, vol. 2, *Medieval and Early Modern Cardiganshire* (forthcoming).
[29] B. P. Evans, 'The family of Mortimer' (University of Wales Ph.D. thesis, 1934); R. R. Davies, 'The Bohun and Lancaster lordships in Wales in the fourteenth and early fifteenth centuries' (University of Oxford D.Phil. thesis, 1965); Ll. B. Smith, 'The lordships of Chirk and Oswestry, 1282–1415' (University of London Ph.D. thesis, 1971); C. P. Lewis, 'English and Norman government and lordship in the Welsh borders, 1039–1087' (University of Oxford D.Phil. thesis, 1985); B. W. Holden, 'The aristocracy of western Herefordshire and the Middle March, 1166–1246' (University of Oxford D.Phil. thesis, 2000); M. Lieberman, 'Shropshire and the March of Wales: the creation of separate identities, c.1070–1283' (University of Oxford D.Phil. thesis, 2004); D. Korngiebel, 'English colonization strategies in Ireland and Wales in the thirteenth and fourteenth centuries' (University of Oxford D.Phil. thesis, 2005).

[30] M. Altschul, *A Baronial Family in Medieval England: The Clares, 1217–1314* (Baltimore, MD, 1965).

[31] R. R. Davies, *Lordship and Society in the March of Wales, 1282–1400* (Oxford, 1978).

[32] R. R. Davies, *The Age of Conquest: Wales 1063–1415* (Oxford, 2000); cf. esp. chs. 4 and 10.

[33] G. W. S. Barrow, *Feudal Britain: The Completion of the Medieval Kingdoms, 1066–1314* (London, 1956).

[34] Professor Sir Rees Davies was the author or editor of many notable landmarks in this field. Cf. R. R. Davies (ed.), *The British Isles, 1100–1500: Comparisons, Contrasts and Connections* (Edinburgh, 1988); see also his Wiles lectures, delivered in Belfast in 1988 and published as *Domination and Conquest: The Experience of Ireland, Scotland and Wales 1100–1300* (Cambridge, 1990); his four presidential addresses to the Royal Historical Society, 'The peoples of Britain and Ireland, 1100–1400. 1. Identities', *TRHS*, 6th ser., 4 (1994), 1–20; 'The peoples of Britain and Ireland, 1100–1400. 2. Names, boundaries and regnal solidarities', *TRHS*, 6th ser., 5 (1995), 1–20; 'The peoples of Britain and Ireland, 1100–1400. 3. Laws and customs', *TRHS*, 6th ser., 6 (1996), 1–23; 'The peoples of Britain and Ireland, 1100–1400. 4. Language and historical mythology', *TRHS*, 6th ser., 7 (1997), 1–24; and his Ford lectures, published as *The First English Empire: Power and Identities in the British Isles 1093–1343* (Oxford, 2000). Other important contributions include R. Frame, *The Political Development of the British Isles, 1100–1400* (Oxford, 1990), with valuable bibliographical essays; A. Grant and K. J. Stringer (eds), *Uniting the Kingdom? The Making of British History* (London, 1995); B. Smith (ed.), *Britain and Ireland 900–1300: Insular Responses to Medieval European Change* (Cambridge, 1999); D. A. Carpenter, *The Struggle for Mastery: Britain 1066–1284* (London, 2003). Among textbooks, the eleven volumes of the *Short Oxford History of the British Isles* show that the 'Atlantic archipelago' perspective is much on the minds of those writing on all periods of British and Irish history since the Romans. The medieval volumes in this series are: T. Charles-Edwards (ed.), *After Rome* (Oxford, 2003); W. Davies (ed.), *From the Vikings to the Normans* (Oxford, 2003); B. Harvey (ed.), *The Twelfth and Thirteenth Centuries. 1066–c.1280* (Oxford, 2001); R. A. Griffiths (ed.), *The Fourteenth and Fifteenth Centuries* (Oxford, 2003).

[35] The following list provides a selection: R. Bartlett and A. MacKay (eds), *Medieval Frontier Societies* (Oxford, 1989); D. Power and N. Standen (eds), *Frontiers in Question: Eurasian Borderlands, 700–1700* (London, 1999); W. Pohl, I. Wood and H. Reimitz (eds), *The Transformation of Frontiers from Late Antiquity to the Carolingians* (Leiden, 2001); D. Abulafia and N. Berend (eds), *Medieval Frontiers: Concepts and Practices* (Aldershot, 2002); P. Bauduin, *La première Normandie (x^e–xie siècles): Sur les frontières de la haute Normandie. Identité et construction d'une principauté* (Caen, 2004); D. Power, *The Norman Frontier in the Twelfth and Early Thirteenth Centuries* (Cambridge, 2004); E. O'Byrne and J. Ní Ghradaigh (eds), *The March in the Medieval West, 1000–1400* (forthcoming).

2

The Making of the March, 1066–1283

The making of the March was a transformation of medieval Britain's political geography. It is also one of the most complex parts of British political history. It has a multiple story line. The campaigns, travails and machinations of nine successive kings of England are integral to it. But so are the exploits of about as many generations of Norman and English barons and Welsh rulers. The Welsh monastic chroniclers assiduously recorded, year by year, every raid, siege, ambush, battle or truce of which news reached their abbeys; but even they could not keep track of all the vicissitudes of Marcher history. Despite this, sketching a chronological framework is an essential part of explaining how the March of Wales was created.

A natural step in grasping the outline of any lengthy historical process is to split that process into phases or chapters. In the case of Marcher history, one can do this in a preliminary but visually striking way by mapping the castles which are thought to have been built in Wales and the borders by 1066 and 1215, and erected or refortified between 1215 and 1300.[1] The contrast between Maps 7 and 8 suggests that, by 1215, a phenomenal effort had already been made to conquer Welsh territory. By then, around 400 castles dotted a country where at most three are thought to have stood a century and a half earlier, in the year of the battle of Hastings. As was argued in Chapter 1, the formative phase of Marcher history spanned the whole period *c.*1067–1283. The maps hint at the scale and pace of that process. They indicate, rightly, that by 1215 almost all of the Welsh valleys and coasts had at one time been raided and occupied, even if only for short periods of time. It is also noticeable that the castles were particularly thick on the ground along the borders and in south Wales, where most of the Marcher lordships survived. As Map 9 shows, this concentration was even clearer in 1300. This suggests, again rightly, that by 1215 the final extent of the March was already being demarcated, and that it changed far less dramatically in the thirteenth century than it had done in the late eleventh and twelfth centuries.

The castles depicted on Maps 7, 8 and 9 are the flotsam and jetsam left by wave upon wave of raids and counter-raids. Mapping them is admittedly a rough-and-ready method. Most of them were erected for military purposes, either by the foreign invaders or by the Welsh – but not all.[2] Some were not in use for very long, others kept playing a military role for generations. Many of these castles were quite small mottes. Others, like Caerffili, were among the most impressive masonry castles in Britain. Nevertheless, comparing and contrasting the maps is very useful. It gives a bird's-eye view of how Norman and English occupation of Welsh territory progressed. Certainly, the castle maps well illustrate how long-drawn-out and piecemeal that process was. They indicate that the parcelling out of roughly half of Wales into Marcher lordships was achieved gradually, bit by bit, and mainly in an uncoordinated fashion, by the effort of individual knights and barons.

At the same time, the castle maps also serve as a reminder that any division of Marcher history into periods will always be, in some measure, an artificial generalization. This is because each lordship, indeed each castle, had its own history. To illustrate this, we might contrast two of the castles with each other, say Pembroke and Builth. Pembroke castle stood in an exceedingly strong position. It was built on what was in the medieval period a narrow ridge protected on either side by the arms of a tidal creek.[3] It was probably first erected in the 1090s, by Arnulf, one of the sons of Roger de Montgomery, the earl of Shrewsbury. Even though the first Welsh attack on it came almost immediately, it never fell. In 1094, it was the only Norman castle bar one in south-west Wales not to be taken.[4] If we may credit Gerald of Wales, the churchman and historian who was born in Pembrokeshire *c.*1146, the castle had a close escape early on. He claims that its constable demoralized a besieging Welsh army by hurling out most of the remaining food (four hogs), thus pretending that the garrison had enough supplies to hold out until reinforcements arrived.[5] This was probably just a family bedtime story about Gerald's grandfather, Gerald of Windsor. Be that as it may, Pembroke castle served as a base, throughout much of the twelfth and thirteenth centuries, for secure Norman and English control over the lowland parts of the old Welsh kingdom of Dyfed. One sign of this is that the Welsh chronicles have almost nothing to say about Pembroke. It was in the hands of the king of England after 1102; by 1130, the castle guarded a royal mint.[6] Like the rest of the March, south-west Wales came under severe pressure from the Welsh during the reign of Stephen of England (1135–54). But Pembroke castle weathered the storm. Indeed, it was Stephen who created the first earl of Pembroke, Gilbert 'Strongbow' de Clare, in 1138.[7] Pembroke castle also played a highly successful role as a relay between England, south Wales and Ireland. This was particularly important to the earls of Pembroke after 1169–70, when they acquired great landed wealth in the Irish kingdom of Leinster.[8] By *c.*1200, the best-known of them, William the Marshal, had added much of the masonry that can still be seen today. The castle remained secure in English hands for the rest of the Middle Ages.

Pembroke castle stands as a monument to an early conquest in Wales which was never reversed. But almost none of the history of the March is so straightforward. Take the extraordinary history of Builth castle, a strategically important motte which guarded a ford on the river Wye.[9] It was probably first built at around the same time as Pembroke castle, in the 1090s, by William I de Braose of southern Normandy. It was then disputed between the Braose family and the Welsh for more than a century. During all that time, it probably remained a fortification of earth and timber, simply because the military threat to it never subsided for long enough for any masonry to be added. The castle was certainly destroyed in 1168 by Rhys ap Gruffudd of Deheubarth, but rebuilt by the Braoses.[10] In 1208, that family fell out of royal favour, and Builth was confiscated by John, the king of England.[11] It continued to be closely beset by the Welsh.[12] Indeed, the Braoses plotted with Llywelyn ab Iorwerth, the Welsh lord of Gwynedd, and recaptured it in 1215.[13] The castle was again attacked by the Welsh in 1217, after the Braoses had become reconciled to Henry III, John's successor.[14] Llywelyn ab Iorwerth himself laid siege to it in 1223. He failed to take it, but in 1228 he captured William V de Braose, who ransomed himself by promising to marry his daughter to Llywelyn's son Dafydd, and to yield the castle and lordship of Builth as her dowry. This plan came to naught. In 1230, Llywelyn found William de Braose in bed with his wife and hanged him.[15] Llywelyn appears to have taken Builth anyway, and to have held it until his death in 1240.[16] In 1242, it was captured for the English crown by John of Monmouth, and probably rebuilt in stone.[17] In 1254, Henry III of England bestowed it upon his son, the future Edward I. But in 1260, Builth castle was besieged, taken through treachery and utterly destroyed by Llywelyn ap Gruffudd, the grandson of Llywelyn ab Iorwerth.[18] In 1267, Henry III conceded Builth to Llywelyn ap Gruffudd in the Treaty of Montgomery.[19] Llywelyn kept Builth until the war of

1276–7, when Edward I, now king of England, captured it and rebuilt it in stone (it is one of the first, if also perhaps the least well-known, of his eight major castles in Wales).[20] In December 1282, it was near Builth castle that Llywelyn was killed;[21] possibly he was on his way to try and bring it, once more, into Welsh hands.

The contrast between castles like Pembroke and Builth needs constantly to be borne in mind when discussing the history of the March as a whole. In identifying the chapters and key dates in Marcher history, it always has to be conceded that what was true in one lordship may have been rather less accurate in another. If the lens is adjusted to a wide enough angle to take in all of the March, then inevitably some important distinctions and variations become blurred. It is also true, however, that the histories of the Marcher castles, and of the lordships which often were centred on them, are not isolated from each other. It is possible to survey even a history as fragmented as that of the March.[22] After all, some questions have to be asked specifically about the bigger picture. Why was Wales only partially conquered between 1066 and 1283? Why was it occupied piecemeal? Why were fewer territorial conquests made in the thirteenth century than in the late eleventh and twelfth centuries?

The three castles which probably already stood on the Herefordshire border by 1066, Richard's Castle, Hereford and Ewyas Harold (from north to south), are among the first mottes built in Britain. They reveal something about the state of the Anglo-Welsh border on the eve of the Norman conquest of England. They are believed to be the work of Normans who had been dispatched to westernmost Herefordshire by Edward the Confessor, the last Anglo-Saxon king but one, who reigned in England from 1042 to 1066. It seems most probable that this was a defensive measure. In particular, it looks like a response to the rise to power of one Gruffudd ap Llywelyn. In 1039, Gruffudd had made himself king of Gwynedd in north Wales. He very possibly caused the death of his predecessor, who had been from an old line of kings of Gwynedd. For the following sixteen years he strove to achieve dominance over Deheubarth, the kingdom of south Wales. Moreover, right from the beginning of his career, he had begun to make his power felt in the English border counties. He defeated a Mercian army in battle at the ford of Rhyd-y-groes on the Severn in 1039, the same year he began his rule over Gwynedd. And in 1052, he attacked the Norman castles on the Herefordshire border. According to the *Anglo-Saxon Chronicle*, 'many

Normans from a castle went up against him, but he routed them and slew many of them, and took great booty'.[23] In 1055, the year in which he finally managed to seize power in south Wales, Gruffudd, aided by an English earl, captured and burned the city and cathedral of Hereford.[24]

The English response to Gruffudd's attacks highlights the nature of the Anglo-Welsh frontier in the eleventh century, and indeed earlier. In 1055, the English assembled an army against Gruffudd, but stopped short of following him into Wales; the English captain, Earl Harold, preferred to negotiate terms. Later, Harold did lead campaigns into Wales, but their object was to seize Gruffudd, not his lands. Late in 1062, Gruffudd escaped by boat from a surprise attack on his stronghold at Rhuddlan on the northern coast.[25] The following year, his rule was cut short abruptly, when Earl Harold led a campaign into Wales, and Gruffudd was betrayed and killed by his own men. Crucially, however, even in the aftermath of Gruffudd's death, the English stopped well short of making any large-scale territorial conquests in Wales (though Harold built himself a short-lived hunting-lodge at Portskewett in Gwent in 1065).

It may be simply that the eleventh-century English lacked the voracious appetite for land which was soon to drive the Normans into Wales. Certainly, in the 1060s, the English had to worry about military threats from Normandy and Scandinavia. But it is also possible that conquering Wales was just something that never occurred to them. By 1066, the boundary between the Welsh and the Anglo-Saxon kingdoms had remained highly stable for centuries.[26] Since the construction of Offa's Dyke just before 800, there had been some English advances and retreats, chiefly along the northern Welsh coast. But overwhelmingly, Anglo-Saxon kings of the ninth and tenth centuries were content with asserting their overlordship over Welsh rulers. This was achieved by punitive raids, but not by campaigns alone. Thus, we hear of symbolic ceremonies designed to demonstrate the exalted status of the English king. In 973, Edgar of England was supposedly rowed across the river Dee by the kings of Wales and of Scotland, while crowds of Welshmen, Englishmen and Scots looked on.[27] Certainly, English kings assumed increasingly grandiloquent titles, such as, in a charter dating to 994, 'I, Ethelred, ruler of the English and governor of the other adjoining nations round about'.[28] It is clearly important that, by the tenth century, the Viking threat had actually forged Anglo-Welsh military alliances. In 893 or 894, for instance, a Danish army was defeated by a joint English and Welsh force at a place called Buttington, which is on the river Severn, almost precisely on the line of Offa's Dyke.[29] During the tenth century, moreover, the priority of the West Saxon kings was the conquest of the Danelaw, that is, of the Scandinavian-occupied parts of former northern and eastern Anglo-Saxon kingdoms (such as Northumbria or Mercia). The Danelaw was incorporated into the tenth-century kingdom of England by conquest; but Wales escaped annexation.

The three mottes on Map 7, then, stood on an ancient frontier. They testified to recent hostilities on that border. But there is no reason to believe that they heralded imminent English or Norman inroads into Wales. Moreover, they had nothing to do with the fateful events of that watershed year in British history, 1066. The historical spotlight for that year has always been, and likely always will be, on the north and south-east of England. On 20 September the earls Edwin and Morcar were defeated by Harold the Hard, king of Norway, at Fulford in Yorkshire. Five days later, the Viking Harold and his men were overcome and killed by Harold, king of England, at Stamford Bridge, also in Yorkshire, a bit further east. On 14 October, the English army, after a forced march to the south of the kingdom, met Duke William of Normandy at Hastings in Sussex. William gained his victory there. Then, after a short period of tactical manoeuvring in south-eastern England, he was crowned king at Westminster Abbey on Christmas Day, and a new, foreign dynasty had taken the throne of England.

Map 8 shows the effect that these momentous events in England ultimately had on Wales. Between 1066 and 1215, castles proliferated at an astonishing rate in that country and on its borders. The mottes of this period are difficult to date closely, and a staggering amount of fieldwork, excavation and historical research still needs to be done before the spread of castles into this part of Britain can be traced in more detail.[30] But the work would be well worth undertaking; to explain castle-building at this period in this part of Britain is to explain how the March of Wales took shape.

It may well be that a great many of the mottes on the second castle map were first built very early on. We know that William fitz Osbern, one of the ablest and most trusted companions of William the Conqueror, built or rebuilt at least four in less than four years, between 1067 and his death in 1071.[31] These four form a line along the borders from Chepstow in the south to Wigmore in northern Herefordshire. But fitz Osbern certainly also led raids into Wales, and he may very well have established some of the castles on or west of the Chepstow–Wigmore line, such as Monmouth, Raglan or Usk.

Fitz Osbern's main border base was Hereford, the town which had been raided by Gruffudd ap Llywelyn only a dozen years before he arrived. As mentioned, fitz Osbern died in 1071 (campaigning in Flanders) but he was succeeded by his son. Moreover, it was not long before other, equally formidable Normans appeared on the Welsh horizon. They were tasked by William the Conqueror with keeping control over whole border counties. Like fitz Osbern, they were all created earls. Roger de Montgomery, another of the few men whom the Conqueror probably knew and trusted since childhood, was installed as earl of Shrewsbury; Hugh d'Avranches, nicknamed 'the Fat', as earl of Chester. Part of the brief these men received was no doubt to keep the peace in the counties. Roger was probably dispatched to Shropshire, possibly as early as 1068, to nip in the bud any joint Anglo-Welsh rebellions like those led by Eadric 'the Wild' in the summer of 1067 and in 1069.[32] But there is every sign that the Norman border earls and their men did not restrict themselves to England for long. As early as 1072, Roger's son Hugh, at the head of a band of raiders, galloped up the Severn valley and into Ceredigion.[33] He and his brothers and friends were probably also responsible for the attacks on Ceredigion and Dyfed in the following year, as well as a further raid into Ceredigion the year after that.[34] Soon afterwards, and definitely before 1081, Earl Roger's right-hand man, Warin, along with Hugh the Fat of Chester, Walter de Lacy, Robert of Rhuddlan and other Norman adventurers, embarked on a plundering campaign as far as the Llŷn peninsula on the western Welsh coast.[35] It is little wonder that the Welsh chronicler's annal for 1102 refers to 'the injuries that the Britons had previously suffered at the hands of Roger [de Montgomery] and of Hugh [his son], which the Britons held in remembrance hidden away in their hearts'.[36]

The early history of Norman occupation of Welsh territory is dominated by the presence of three powerful border earldoms with bases at Hereford, Shrewsbury and Chester. Whether or not William the Conqueror intended his border earls to play a defensive or an offensive role is a moot point. None of these earls were men to waste an opportunity, and they brought a great number of like-minded followers in their train. Hugh the Fat, indeed, left much of the raiding from Chester into north Wales to his cousin, Robert de Tilleul 'of Rhuddlan'. As for the sons of Roger de Montgomery, all but one of them were in the same predicament: as younger sons they could not hope for any share in the family patrimony. Their only chance at moving up in the world was to grab any land they could get, by any means they could get away with.

Their early raids into Wales were plainly exploratory; and it has already been mentioned that it was one of them, Arnulf, who first built Pembroke castle. William the Conqueror made no attempt at conquering Wales. His only known personal venture into the country occurred in 1081, when he went on what one Welsh annal refers to as a 'pilgrimage' to St David's.[37] This was no doubt in part an assertion of his military superiority and claim to overlordship. Domesday Book recorded five years later that one 'Riset of Wales' owed the Conqueror an annual tribute of £40. It is possible that this was Rhys ap Tewdwr, who in 1081 had just become ruler of south Wales.[38] However, it was certainly not Wales that topped the Conqueror's agenda, but the consolidation of his rule over England. It was for this very reason that, when the Norman raids into Welsh territory began, they were launched from several bases in parallel. William made an important contribution to the shape of later Marcher history by creating his three border earldoms, and by allowing them free rein in Wales. Indeed, it is no exaggeration to say that, during his reign, the general pattern of Marcher history was first established. Piecemeal conquests by individual barons, not attempted total conquest by the king of England, were to be the norm until 1282–3.

Even so, the first onslaught on Wales was fearful. By 1086, the border earls and their men were claiming Welsh territories as far away as Arwystli; the £40 tribute from north Wales was owed not by a Welsh ruler, but by Robert of Rhuddlan.[39] But the border earls also met with severe setbacks. Two of their earldoms did not, perhaps could not, last long. In 1075, fitz Osbern's son rebelled against the king and forfeited the earldom of Hereford; in 1098, Hugh de Montgomery, by then second earl of Shrewsbury, was killed by Vikings on Anglesey; in 1102, his brother Robert, the third earl, rebelled and forfeited the earldom of Shrewsbury. The earldom of Chester survived, but it came into royal custody in 1101 because Hugh the Fat died, leaving a minor as an heir. The border earldoms were the bases from which some of the first Marcher enterprises were launched. But they did not monopolize the initiative for long.

This was partly due to forfeiture and minority. However, it was also because another landmark in Marcher history came in 1093, 'when Rhys ap Tewdwr, king of Deheubarth, was slain by the French who were inhabiting Brycheiniog'.[40] The violent death of the leading Welsh figure in the south of the country was clearly significant; it may even be that it opened the floodgates to a new wave of incursions by Normans who were in no way connected to any of the border earls. Rather they tended to owe everything directly to the first Norman kings of England. Thus, the man leading the assault on Brycheiniog, Bernard de Neufmarché, had only arrived in Herefordshire between 1086 and 1088, having received land there from either William I (d.1087) or William II (king 1087–1100); Robert fitz Hamo, who spearheaded the Norman advance into the Welsh kingdom of Morgannwg, laying the ground-stone for Glamorgan lordship, was the son of a royal steward. William II, like his father the Conqueror, helped shape the March principally by deciding whom to send to Wales.

Yet another reason why the initiative passed from the border earldoms was that the years 1094–6 saw the first country-wide uprising of the Welsh against Norman occupation. Two campaigns led by William II to Wales, in 1094 and 1097, achieved very little, not least because the Welsh prudently melted away into the hills before his armies.[41] The roll-call of castles which were overrun and destroyed in the 1090s reflects both the Welsh success and the remarkable extent of the earlier Norman advance. There was hardly a part of Wales that was not involved in these wars: Welsh attacks on Norman castles in Gwynedd, Ceredigion and Dyfed in 1094 were followed by Norman reprisals on Gower, Cydweli and Ystrad Tywi in 1095; the following year, the Welsh targeted the Normans in Brycheiniog, Gwent and Gwynllŵg.[42] Thirty years after Hastings, the Welsh faced Normans virtually everywhere in their country.

It was indicated above that, by 1215, the extent of the March had already largely been determined; but that stage was yet some way off in 1100. The Welsh attacks of the 1090s had demonstrated the vulnerability of the Norman conquest territories, particularly in the north of the country. They had made it clear that the complete conquest of Wales would have to be achieved by different means. But that continued not to be a priority of the kings of England in the first half of the twelfth century. Under Henry I (1100–35), and to a considerable extent due to him, the nascent Marcher lordships were consolidated and indeed expanded. Henry was remembered by the Welsh chroniclers as 'the man who had tamed all the chieftains of the island of Britain through his might and power . . . the man against whom none can contend save God Himself'.[43] He cemented this reputation by divide-and-rule tactics, by establishing royal bases at Pembroke and Carmarthen, by placing reliable men in charge of the conquest lordships and not least by leading campaigns against the Welsh in 1114 and 1121.[44] However, the reign of his successor Stephen (1135–54) was plagued by civil war in England, and marked by a significant crumbling of Norman and English power in Wales.

The contrast between the two reigns is most striking in the case of Ceredigion. During Henry I's reign it began to look as if this region on the western coast of Wales would become a Marcher lordship. But by the end of Stephen's reign that possibility seemed very remote indeed. Ceredigion had seen its share of Norman raids by 1100. But its occupation only began in earnest in 1110, when Henry I apparently launched Gilbert fitz Richard into west Wales with the words: 'You were always ... seeking of me a portion of the territory of the Britons. I will now give you Cadwgan's territory. Go and take possession of it.'[45] Gilbert and his men would appear to have seized Ceredigion piece by piece; almost all the mottes they built there guarded one commote.[46] The Clare conquest of Ceredigion also shows particularly well how much the Norman and English conquerors relied on their knights. Gilbert himself and his son Richard built the castles to guard Cardigan, Aberystwyth and Ystrad Meurig. But the other newly erected castles in Ceredigion were named after Gilbert's men: Razo, Stephen, Humphrey, Richard de la Mare and Walter del Bec.[47]

That Henry I himself led two campaigns to Wales shows that the conquest lordships there were by no means entirely secure during his reign. Nevertheless, the focus of the Welsh annals during these years is more on the gruesome family feuding by which the dynasty of Powys was decimating itself at the time. A period of about six months elapsed after the death of Henry I before the collapse of Norman power began in earnest.[48] But in Ceredigion it was nearly complete. Here the sons of Gruffudd ap Cynan, king of Gwynedd (d.1137), led the rout. Cardigan was the only castle the Welsh did not capture in a series of fell swoops in 1136–8.[49]

The evidence is too skimpy to compare the Welsh military actions during Stephen's reign at all fully with those of the 1090s. The Welsh raids of the later period were most strikingly successful in Ceredigion. True, by 1149, Madog ap Maredudd of Powys was in possession of Oswestry castle, one of the first castles the Normans built on the Welsh border after 1066. However, it is far from clear whether Madog captured Oswestry castle by military force or whether he acquired it by negotiation.[50] It should be noted, moreover, that the English advance seems not to have been reversed, or even halted, either in Glamorgan or in Elfael and Maelienydd in the central March. Brecon and Abergavenny lordships appear to have escaped largely unscathed. During Stephen's reign, not all of the progress made by the Normans and the English under Henry I was reversed.

Moreover, there must have been some apprehensive speculation in Wales, at the accession of Henry II in 1154, about how far the military pendulum would swing during his reign, and in which direction. Henry had vast military resources at his disposal. The man crowned king of England in 1154 was already duke of Normandy and of Aquitaine and count of Anjou. Moreover, he came to the throne patently determined to restore his realm to the state in which his grandfather, Henry I, had left it. It was a few years before he turned his attention to Wales. But his military expeditions against Gwynedd in 1157 and Deheubarth in 1158 and 1163 forced two of the chief Welsh rulers, Owain Gwynedd and Rhys ap Gruffudd, to do fealty. They were also constrained to yield territory, notably Englefield (Welsh: Tegeingl), the area between the Clwyd and the Dee, which they had captured during Stephen's reign. Oswestry, too, was returned to its English lord. Henry II's initial successes did not, however, produce the desired effect of permanently subduing the Welsh. Quite the contrary. In the words of the chronicler, in 1164 'all the Welsh made a pact to drive out the garrisons of the French, and that united all together'.[51] Henry II, on hearing of this, amassed an army and fleet from England, Scotland, Ireland and France. Preparations for his campaign took over a year; he may have been determined to conquer Wales.[52] However, in 1165 Henry decided to lead the expedition from Oswestry on the Shropshire border across the Berwyn mountain range. No doubt he hoped to gain a decisive advantage over the joint Welsh force encamped at Corwen on the other side. It was a risky operation, and it ended in disaster. Once Henry had reached the top of the mountain (having been harried by the Welsh along the way), he was forced to encamp there for several days, probably because of supply problems. Worse, 'he was oppressed by a mighty tempest of wind and exceeding great torrents of rain'. In the end Henry was forced to retreat back to Shropshire without having engaged the main Welsh force at all.[53]

This in itself might not have been enough to discourage Henry II from further ventures into Wales. But in the late 1160s and early 1170s a small number of Marchers joined forces with an exiled Irish king and began, with startling success, to capture towns and provinces in Ireland. Moreover, in 1173–4 Henry II's sons, allied with the kings of Scotland and of France, rebelled against him. These events had an indirect but lasting effect on Marcher history. In 1171–2, Henry crossed over to Ireland in order to secure the submissions of Irish kings and impose a measure of control over the Marchers there.[54] His Irish expedition meant two trips through south Wales, and he took the opportunity to make truces with the Welsh princes of Gwynedd and the Lord Rhys of Deheubarth.[55] In keeping with this more conciliatory approach to the Welsh, he began to lean heavily on the Marchers. In 1175 he delivered a sharp reminder to William, earl of Gloucester, William de Braose 'and other barons of that land' that he would brook no infringement of the truces with the Welsh.[56] The earl of Gloucester was ordered to restore Caerleon to its Welsh ruler. William de Braose was relieved of his duties as lieutenant in south Wales for the part he allegedly played in a massacre of Welshmen at Abergavenny. In 1179, Roger Mortimer of Wigmore was incarcerated because his men had killed Cadwallon ap Madog, the ruler of Maelienydd. Not only did this blatantly disregard Henry II's recent directives; Cadwallon had in fact been granted a royal safe conduct on his way back to Wales from Henry II's court. The king's retribution was harsh. Roger's castle at Cymaron was confiscated, and a number of his men were executed or punished.[57]

The accords of 1171–2 ushered in a spell of about forty years during which no king of England led a campaign to Wales. The pace of Marcher enterprise was slackening anyway. This was partly because specific Marcher families had already staked their claims to the southern coastlands and a number of the eastern valleys. At around the same time, many of the land-hungry Marchers in Wales began to be lured away by the ample prospects which seemed to have opened up in Ireland. Moreover, during the 1170s and 1180s, a number of the keenest conquerors died without leaving a male heir, their lands passing temporarily into royal custody: notably William, earl of Gloucester, lord of Glamorgan; Richard 'Strongbow', the earl of Pembroke and lord of Chepstow and of Usk, who had been involved in the earliest incursions into Ireland; and William de Beaumont, earl of Warwick and lord of Gower. It was during this period, in 1188, that Gerald went on his expedition around Wales, accompanying Baldwin, the archbishop of Canterbury, on a mission to recruit Welshmen and Marchers for the Third Crusade. Richard I, the 'Lionheart', was too busy crusading and being held hostage in Germany to pay any attention to Wales whatsoever. It was only after he had been succeeded by his younger brother, John, and John had lost Normandy in 1204, that an English king once again led armies to Wales, as happened twice in 1211 and once in 1212.

Such is the background to the situation prevailing in the March in 1215, the year of Magna Carta, the year by which some 400 castles had been built in Wales and the borders. As mentioned earlier, this document refers to a 'March' between England and Wales. By the time the Great

Charter was sealed by the reluctant John, it had also become common for the king's clerks to speak of 'barons of the March'. That such terms had been coined is in itself revealing. It suggests that the conquests in Wales were considered to be irreversible. But it also indicates an acceptance that Wales was to remain only partly conquered.[58]

It is understandable why such a conclusion should have been reached. On the other hand, while a group among the king's barons were apparently identified as the Marchers, the barons who held lands on the Welsh borders and in Wales in 1215 did not form a very neat category. For one thing, all of the lords of the chief castles also held lands elsewhere, most commonly in England and on the Continent or, from about 1170, in Ireland. But the balance between these concerns varied widely. Again, a brief comparison may serve to illustrate this, say between Hugh Mortimer, the lord of Wigmore, and William the Marshal, the earl of Pembroke and lord of Chepstow. In 1215, the young Hugh Mortimer had just inherited Wigmore, on the borders between Herefordshire and the Welsh kingdom of Maelienydd, from his father. He also had succeeded to English lands in central Wessex, Yorkshire and Lincolnshire as well as the family inheritance in eastern Normandy. But he can have been in no doubt that Wigmore castle, even though it lay furthest to the west of all his newly acquired dominions, was where the heart of his family inheritance lay. Wigmore castle had first been granted to his great-great-grandfather, Ralph, around 1075. Ever since, for five generations, Hugh's ancestors had been fighting to gain control over Welsh territory to the west of the castle. His grandfather and father were both buried at Wigmore priory, which had been established by his forebears. Hugh's father, Roger, had been imprisoned for killing a Welsh prince. In 1199, Roger Mortimer made a grant of land to an abbey in Wales. As was conventional at the time, he made it for the souls of his family. But remarkably, he also made it for the souls of his men and of 'those who died in the conquest of Maelienydd'.[59]

Not all barons of the March were Marchers to the extent that the Mortimers were. William the Marshal was born in England in around 1146 and died in 1219.[60] The Marshal family held land in Wiltshire and Berkshire, but none on the Welsh borders or in Wales. In any case, William the Marshal had three older brothers, so he had to make his own fortune. He became the quintessential self-made man of the international chivalric world centred on twelfth-century northern France. Having grown up in foster-parentage in England and Normandy, he succeeded brilliantly in winning renown and fortune, by participating in tournaments and by attaching himself to various noble households, including that of Henry the Young King (d.1183), the son of Henry II of England. William became a Marcher lord by stages, through the patronage of the kings of England. In 1188, Henry II offered him the marriage to Isabel, daughter and heiress of Richard de Clare, also known as Strongbow. This gave the Marshal Chepstow, which, like the Mortimer castle of Wigmore, had been built more than a century earlier by William fitz Osbern. William's marriage to Strongbow's heiress also meant that he acquired a claim to lands in Ireland, for, as noted, Strongbow had been one of the first English conquerors in that country. In 1199, William the Marshal was created earl of Pembroke, as a reward for supporting John's successful bid to succeed Richard the Lionheart as king of England. With the title earl of Pembroke came tenure of Pembroke lordship in south-western Wales. But the young Hugh Mortimer was a Marcher born and bred. William the Marshal was not.

The roles played by the Mortimers and the Marshal in 1215 compare interestingly. There was no difference in terms of their political allegiance: Mortimer and the Marshal both supported John, the king of England. But William the Marshal was the king's chief lay negotiator at Oxford in January 1215; in July, the Marshal was sent to the March to deal with the problem of some other Marcher barons and Llywelyn ab Iorwerth, who had captured Shrewsbury in May 1215. After King John died in 1216, the Marshal was elected Guardian of England, and ran the kingdom until he died of old age in 1219. William the Marshal's life is commemorated in a verse biography, composed during the 1220s. This is almost 20,000 lines long, and is one of the few biographies that survive for any laymen of medieval Europe, including kings.[61] By contrast, we would not even know which side Hugh Mortimer was on in 1215 if it had not been for the chance survival of a single letter identifying John's supporters and opponents in the March. William the Marshal was a much bigger fish than Mortimer; the Welsh borders were just one of the Marshal's many preoccupations. In this sense, Mortimer and the Marshal represent two very different kinds of Marcher lords.

Essentially, what separates the situation on Maps 8 and 9 is the long reign of Henry III, who came to the English throne as a 9-year-old in 1216 and died in 1272. On the eve of Edward I's Welsh wars of 1276–7 and 1282–3, the March was in many respects similar to what it had been in 1215. To be sure, in terms of its lords the March was hardly recognizable. A great many of the old families had become extinct in the male line. Most spectacularly, the last two of the five sons of William the Marshal died in

1245, and the Marshal inheritance was divided up between co-heiresses. The Braoses had failed in the male line in 1230, when William V was hanged by Llywelyn ab Iorwerth; gone, too, were the families of Lacy (1241), fitz Baderon of Monmouth (1257) and Clifford (1263).[62] The newcomers included Bohun (who replaced the Braoses at Brecon in 1241), Bigod at Chepstow and Valence at Pembroke. On the other hand, some of the old families survived and even prospered. The Clares of Glamorgan added Caerleon and Usk (or Lower Gwent) to their possessions after the Marshals failed in 1245.[63] The Corbets of Caus were descended in direct male line from one of the companions of Roger de Montgomery, the first earl of Shrewsbury, and well aware of it. In about 1250, Thomas Corbet had refused to pay the king baronial relief 'because', he declared, 'none of his five predecessors had ever paid it'.[64] The Mortimers, of course, continued to hold Wigmore.

Both the new families and the old dynasties continued to have important interests outside the March. Even the Mortimers acquired lands in England and Ireland in the thirteenth century, mostly through making advantageous marriages. It was by marriage, similarly, that the Fitzalans, who were lords of Clun and Oswestry, two Marcher lordships just to the north of the Mortimer lordship of Wigmore, became earls of Arundel (and therefore the chief landholders in Sussex) in the thirteenth century. This inevitably led to absenteeism and, it could be claimed, meant that the lords of the chief Marcher castles ceased to be true Marcher lords. Increasingly, the landholders whose main interests lay in the March were the knightly families and minor castellans, those who often owed military services such as castle-guard at the chief Marcher castles, or who acted as local officials – stewards, constables or bailiffs – for absentee lords. For such families, the March remained a land of opportunity. Even if great conquests in Wales lay beyond their means, the Audleys, for instance, made a striking career for themselves as royal emissaries to Welsh lords and later as justiciars of Chester.

The Anglo-Welsh détente which began around 1172 was perhaps bound to end sooner or later. Hostilities between the English and the Welsh did not cease completely during the reigns of Henry II and Richard I.[65] That a decisive break came in 1211 was clearly linked to the Continental wars which had, by 1205, caused John of England to lose almost all his French lands. This robbed the kings of England of a good deal of military clout. On the other hand, it also undoubtedly concentrated more of their attention on the British Isles in general, and Wales in particular. John led campaigns against Scotland in 1209, against Ireland in 1210 and against Wales in 1211 (twice) and in 1212. However, there were also a number of reasons why the extent of the March changed very little during Henry III's long reign. One was the hegemonic role within Wales which the rulers of Gwynedd assumed. In 1211–12, the failure of John's campaigns against the lord of Gwynedd, Llywelyn ab Iorwerth, greatly strengthened that ruler's authority in Wales. Llywelyn pressed his advantage with a series of military successes, notably the occupation of Shrewsbury in 1215. By 1218, when Henry III's minority government conceded his conquests to him, albeit grudgingly and on a temporary basis, he had extended his influence over virtually all the native rulers of Wales.[66]

Already before Llywelyn's remarkable rise to supremacy within native Wales, it was becoming increasingly difficult for individual Marchers to make progress against the Welsh. In 1196, the year before he died, the Lord Rhys, who had ruled Deheubarth since almost the beginning of Henry II's reign, had inflicted a painful defeat on Mortimer.[67] Once Llywelyn ab Iorwerth had reached the height of his power, the Marchers were largely reduced to playing a defensive role. Offensives might still occur at propitious moments. In 1223, William Marshal the younger used the diversion provided by a successful royal campaign in order to seize Cilgerran castle. But Llywelyn's sweeping raids in 1231 and 1233 against Marcher castles from the Shropshire borders to Gower and Cydweli delivered powerful demonstrations of the prevailing balance of power. In 1231 he is said to have 'ground down the lands and possessions of the barons who lived on the borders of Wales with a terrifying raid of destruction'.[68]

The Marchers, then, never regained the momentum that had carried their eleventh- and twelfth-century predecessors to the furthest reaches of Wales. On the other hand, nor did they lose much ground to the Welsh. For one thing, after Llywelyn ab Iorwerth died in 1240, the web of loyalties he had spun throughout native Wales began rapidly to unravel, chiefly due to the rivalry between his two sons, the half-brothers Gruffudd and Dafydd. Henry III exploited the situation with resounding success, seizing several important districts in north Wales and Llanbadarn in west Wales and taking back direct control of Carmarthen and Cardigan. Moreover, between 1237 and 1241 the crown had annexed the county of Cheshire. From this position of landed strength, and buoyed by the demise of Llywelyn ab Iorwerth's sons in 1244 and 1246, Henry III quelled a Welsh revolt in 1245 and proceeded to implement a highly effective divide-and-rule policy in order to gain the upper hand in native Wales for another decade.[69]

The more enterprising among the Marchers made the most of the situation. The Mortimers, notably, once again began pursuing territorial gains in Maelienydd.[70] But the initiative was not to remain with them for long. Llywelyn ap Gruffudd, grandson of Llywelyn ab Iorwerth, ended the period of dynastic strife in Gwynedd in 1255, and in the following year repossessed the northern Welsh territories which had been conceded to Henry III in the 1247 Treaty of Woodstock. His timing was immaculate, for over the period 1258–65 relations between the English king and his barons deteriorated to the point of civil war once more. Llywelyn made all the territorial gains he could during this period, notably to the south of Gwynedd and in the middle March. What is more, in 1267 he had these confirmed to him, along with an acknowledgement of the title prince of Wales, in the Treaty of Montgomery with Henry III.

From the point of view of the Marchers, this meant a reversion to the defensive role they had begun to play earlier in the century. The motivation for further military action lay not so much in the prospect of gaining landed wealth but in protecting that which had already been conquered. The Clare lords of Glamorgan, for instance, imprisoned the lord of Senghennydd, an upland commote to the north of Cardiff. In 1268 they began work on a vast masonry castle at Caerffili to consolidate their domination over upland Morgannwg. But for men of lesser means, even defending Marcher properties proved too much of a challenge. Already earlier in Henry III's reign, Thomas ap Madog had exchanged the manor of Kinnerley on the Shropshire borders with James Audley because 'he', Thomas, 'could not hold his own against the Welsh'.[71] A number of disputes between Marcher lords and their Welsh neighbours, such as that between the Corbet lords of Caus and the Welsh lords of southern Powys, simmered on until they were eventually brought before the king of England for adjudication.

Such was the protracted period of consolidation in Marcher history which led up to the creation of the fully fledged March described in the last chapter, and illustrated by Maps 1 and 9. Throughout the thirteenth century, the English crown had tipped the military balance between the Marchers and the Welsh. It was fitting, therefore, that the finishing touches to the March were added by Edward I. Only four years elapsed between that king's accession in 1272 and his initial campaign in Wales. In 1279, he created his first Marcher lordships, Ceri and Cedewain, for Roger Mortimer of Wigmore. The stage was set for 1282–3 and the establishment of the Principality and the 'new' Marcher lordships in north Wales.

The mushrooming of castles along the Welsh borders and south Wales, then, does suggest a valid division into periods of Marcher history between 1067 and 1300. Moreover, it can be refined further without doing too much injustice to the differences between the various conquest lordships. Much of the first century of Marcher history followed the rhythm set by the reigns of the Norman kings of England: William I and William II (1066–1100), Henry I (1100–35), and Stephen (1135–54). The reign of the first Plantagenet, Henry II (1154–89), falls into two parts as far as the March is concerned. The first, confident phase ended with the debacle of 1165. The second was characterized by a much more accommodating approach to the Welsh, and a less forgiving attitude towards the Marchers. There followed a long spell of relative peace, during which no English king led a campaign to Wales. This was ended by John's expeditions of 1211 and 1212. As for the thirteenth century after 1212, one might opt for the reigns of the rulers of Gwynedd to divide Marcher history into chapters: Llywelyn ab Iorwerth (d.1240); an interregnum during which Henry III of England dominated Wales (1240–56); and Llywelyn ap Gruffudd (1256–82). The history of the March does not quite fit into the history of native Wales or the history of England; but it is closely tied to both.

The questions asked above were: why was Wales only partially conquered between 1066 and 1283? Why was it occupied piecemeal? Why were fewer territorial conquests made in the thirteenth century than in the late eleventh and twelfth centuries? To try and give the shortest possible answers, much of the earliest history of the March was shaped by the initiative of land-hungry knights and barons. The role of the kings of England should be given its due. But overall, in the period between the Norman conquest of England and the English conquest of Wales, the kings did little to change the piecemeal way in which Welsh territory was seized. Partly this was because they viewed Wales as a welcome source of territories with which to reward loyal service, particularly after c.1100, when such territories had become rare in England. Partly it was because when the kings did lead really large-scale campaigns to Wales, they failed to achieve the permanent occupation of native Wales. From the later twelfth century, and particularly in the thirteenth, the role of the kings of England became crucial in determining the advance and retreat of English power in Wales, particularly due to the leadership provided in native Wales by the princes of Gwynedd. The wars of 1282–3 ended a period of stalemate between the Marcher lords and the Welsh rulers which had lasted for more than a century and during which the Marcher lordships were consolidated.

The March of Wales was over two hundred years in the making. This goes a long way towards explaining why it survived for as long as it did. By the time Edward I led his final campaigns to Wales in 1282–3, there were castles and lordships in that country which had first been established six generations previously. The idea that Wales was a divided country had become firmly entrenched. The existence of *Marchia Wallie* was accepted as a given by 1200 and was to be further perpetuated by the Statute of Rhuddlan in 1284. Such, it might be suggested for the time being, are the general outlines of Marcher history. It remains to be seen how far this bird's-eye view will be changed by the work of future historians and archaeologists.

Notes

[1] See Maps 7, 8 and 9. The maps are based on A. H. A. Hogg and D. J. C. King, 'Early castles in Wales and the marches', *Arch. Camb.*, 112 (1963), 77–124; idem, 'Masonry castles in Wales and the marches: a list', *Arch. Camb.*, 116 (1967), 71–132; idem, 'Castles in Wales and the marches: additions and corrections', *Arch. Camb.*, 119 (1970), 119–24, Map 8 also shows castles dated to before 1217 in RCAHMW, *An Inventory of the Ancient Monuments in Glamorgan*, vol. 3, part 1a, *Medieval Secular Monuments: The Early Castles. From the Norman Conquest to 1217* (London, 1991), Map 9 also shows castles dated to between 1217 and 1300 in RCAHMW, *An Inventory of the Ancient Monuments in Glamorgan*, vol. 3, part 1b, *Medieval Secular Monuments: The Later Castles. From 1217 to the Present* (Llandudno, 2000).

[2] Cf. C. L. H. Coulson, *Castles in Medieval Society* (Oxford, 2003), on non-military uses of castles.

[3] D. J. C. King, 'Pembroke castle', *Arch. Camb.*, 127 (1979 for 1978), 77.

[4] *Brut*, pp. 34–5.

[5] Gerald of Wales, *The Journey through Wales/The Description of Wales*, trans. L. Thorpe (London, 1978), pp. 148–9 (*Journey*, i, 12).

[6] *Brut*, pp. 46–7, 48–9; *Pipe Roll 31 Henry I*, ed. J. Hunter (1833, repr. in facs. London, 1929), p. 136.

[7] *The Ecclesiastical History of Orderic Vitalis*, ed. and trans. M. Chibnall (6 vols, Oxford, 1969–80), vi, 520–1.

[8] King, 'Pembroke castle', p. 77.

[9] C. J. Spurgeon, 'Builth Castle', *Brycheiniog*, 18 (1978–79), 47–59.

[10] *Annales Cambrie*, ed. J. Williams ab Ithel (RS, 1860), s.a. 1169.

[11] *Brut*, pp. 186–7.

[12] Ibid., pp. 190–1.

[13] Ibid., pp. 202–3; Lloyd, *History of Wales*, pp. 644–5.

[14] Ibid., pp. 214–15.

15. *Brut*, pp. 228–9; *Mon. Ang.*, iv, 615; vi, 134; Matthew Paris, *Chron. maj.*, iii, 194.
16. *Calendar of Ancient Correspondence Concerning Wales*, ed. J. G. Edwards (Cardiff, 1935), pp. 35–6, 53.
17. *Brut*, pp. 238–9.
18. Ibid., pp. 250–1.
19. *Littere Wallie*, ed. J. G. Edwards (Cardiff, 1940), p. 2.
20. *Brut*, pp. 264–5. Edward I began building Builth, Flint, Rhuddlan and Aberystwyth in 1277, Conway and Caernarvon in 1283, Harlech in 1285 and Beaumaris in 1295.
21. *Calendar of Ancient Correspondence*, ed. Edwards, pp. 83–4.
22. See, for instance, Davies, *Age of Conquest*, chs 4 and 10.
23. *EHD*, ii, 220.
24. Ibid., pp. 222–3.
25. Ibid., p. 140; Lloyd, *History of Wales*, pp. 369–70.
26. W. Davies, *Patterns of Power in Early Wales* (Oxford, 1990), ch. 5.
27. D. Thornton, 'Edgar and the eight kings, AD 973: *textus et dramatis personae*', *Early Medieval Europe*, 10 (2001), 49–79; J. Barrow, 'Chester's earliest regatta? Edgar's Dee-rowing revisited', *Early Medieval Europe*, 10 (2001), 81–93.
28. *EHD*, i, 228, n. 1; 569.
29. Ibid., i, 203–4.
30. But cf. already the splendid volumes on the castles of Glamorgan, RCAHMW, *An Inventory of the Ancient Monuments in Glamorgan: The Early Castles* and *The Later Castles*; and the classic study of Hen Domen Montgomery, R. Higham and P. A. Barker, *Hen Domen Montgomery: A Timber Castle on the English–Welsh Border. A Final Report* (Oxford, 2000).
31. William is recorded in Domesday Book as having built the castles of Chepstow, also called Strigoil (DB 162), of Clifford (DB 183) and of Wigmore (DB 183); and as having refortified Ewyas Harold (DB 186).
32. C. P. Lewis, 'The early earls of Norman England', *Anglo-Norman Studies*, 13 (1990), 219–20; *Regesta regum Anglo-Normannorum: The Acta of William I (1066–1087)*, ed. D. Bates (Oxford, 1998), no. 181, p. 599 (11 May 1068) witnessed by Roger of Montgomery, earl of Shrewsbury.
33. *Annales Cambrie*, p. 26.
34. *Brut*, pp. 28–9; J. F. A. Mason, 'Roger de Montgomery and his sons (1067–1102)', *TRHS*, 5th ser., 13 (1963), 12.
35. *The History of Gruffudd ap Cynan*, ed. and trans. A. Jones (Manchester, 1910), pp. 122–5; *Historia Gruffud vab Kenan*, ed. D. Simon Evans (Cardiff, 1977), pp. 12–13; *A Mediaeval Prince of Wales: The Life of Gruffudd ap Cynan*, ed. and trans. D. Simon Evans (Felinfach, 1990), pp. 34, 65; *Vita Griffini Filii Conani: The Medieval Latin Life of Gruffudd ap Cynan*, ed. and trans. P. Russell (Cardiff, 2005), §16 (pp. 66–7).
36. *Brut*, pp. 44–5.
37. Ibid., pp. 30–1.
38. DB 179; Lloyd, *History of Wales*, p. 394.
39. DB 269.
40. *Brut*, pp. 32–3.

[41] *Brut*, pp. 34–7.
[42] Ibid., pp. 32–7.
[43] Ibid., pp. 90–1 (annal for 1116).
[44] R. R. Davies, 'Henry I and Wales', in H. Mayr-Harting and R. I. Moore (eds), *Studies in Medieval History Presented to R. H. C. Davis* (London, 1985), pp. 132–47.
[45] *Brut*, pp. 70–1.
[46] Edwards, 'The Normans and the Welsh March', 164–8.
[47] Davies, *Age of Conquest*, pp. 88–91; D. J. C. King, 'The castles of Ceredigion', *Ceredigion*, 3/1 (1956), 50–69.
[48] D. Crouch, 'The March and the Welsh kings', in E. King (ed), *The Anarchy of King Stephen's Reign* (Oxford, 1994), pp. 256–89.
[49] Davies, *Age of Conquest*, p. 51.
[50] *Brut*, pp. 128–9; *Annales Cambrie*, p. 44; cf. Lieberman, 'Shropshire and the March of Wales', p. 98; D. Stephenson, 'Madog ap Maredudd: *rex Powissensium*', *WHR* (forthcoming). I would like to thank Dr Stephenson for kindly sending me a draft of this article.
[51] *Brut*, pp. 144–5.
[52] Davies, *Age of Conquest*, p. 53. Cf. P. Latimer, 'Henry II's campaign against the Welsh in 1165', *WHR*, 14 (1988), 523–52.
[53] *Brut*, pp. 144–7.
[54] Among those Marchers were several of the kinsmen of Gerald of Wales as well as Richard 'Strongbow' de Clare, to whom Henry appears to have granted the title of earl of Pembroke on this occasion. Cf. M. T. Flanagan, *Irish Society, Anglo-Norman Settlers, Angevin Kingship: Interactions in Ireland in the Late Twelfth Century* (Oxford, 1989), ch. 4.
[55] *Brut*, pp. 154–9.
[56] Davies, *Domination and Conquest*, pp. 74–5; *Gesta regis Henrici Secundi*, ed. W. Stubbs (2 vols, RS, 1867), i, 92.
[57] Davies, *Age of Conquest*, p. 275; Lloyd, *History of Wales*, p. 567; *Brut*, pp. 168–9; Ralph of Diss, *Opera historica*, ed. W. Stubbs (2 vols, RS, 1876), i, 437; *Pipe Roll 25 Henry II, 1178–9* (PRS, 28), p. 39.
[58] Davies, *Age of Conquest*, p. 272.
[59] Cf. 'An early charter of the abbey of Cwmhir', ed. B. G. Charles, *The Transactions of the Radnorshire Society*, 40 (1970), 68–73; and comments in J. B. Smith, 'The middle March in the thirteenth century', *BBCS*, 24 (1970–2), 80–1.
[60] For a biography of the Marshal cf. D. Crouch, *William Marshal: Court, Career and Chivalry in the Angevin Empire 1147–1219* (London, 1990).
[61] *History of William Marshal*, ed. A. J. Holden, trans. S. Gregory, historical notes by D. Crouch (3 vols, Anglo-Norman Text Society Occasional Publications, 4–6, London, 2002–6).
[62] Davies, *Lordship and Society*, p. 37.
[63] Altschul, *The Clares*, p. 50 and n. 124.
[64] PRO/TNA E 368/24, m. 12v; cf. R. W. Eyton, *Antiquities of Shropshire* (12 vols, London, 1854–60), vii, 24.

[65] Cf., for instance, J. Gillingham, 'Henry II, Richard I and the Lord Rhys', *Peritia*, 10 (1996), 225–36; repr. in idem, *The English in the Twelfth Century*, pp. 59–68.

[66] For the series of three agreements between Llywelyn ab Iorwerth and Henry III's minority government cf. *AWR*, nos. 240–2.

[67] *Brut*, pp. 176–7.

[68] Roger of Wendover, *Chronica, sive flores historiarum*, ed. H. O. Coxe (4 vols, London, 1841–4), iv, 221.

[69] Davies, *Age of Conquest*, pp. 300–7.

[70] Lloyd, *History of Wales*, p. 697; Matthew Paris, *Chron. maj.*, iv, 319–20; Davies, *Age of Conquest*, p. 276.

[71] *Calendar of Inquisitions Miscellaneous, 1219–1307* (London, 1916), p. 322, no. 1059; Davies, *Age of Conquest*, p. 280.

3

The Social and Economic March, 1067–1300

Warfare could have devastating effects on the largely agrarian economies of medieval Europe. In the short term, peasants suffered hardship when their crops were burned. Such economic attrition was a tactic to which medieval captains commonly resorted. It was a way of depriving enemies of supplies.[1] Armed conflict also prevented crops being harvested and brought to market in the towns. Where it was protracted, warfare sometimes stopped production altogether. The Hundred Years War between England and France (1337–1453) largely brought wine-growing in the area around Bordeaux to a standstill. Peasants there found they could sow wheat during the brief interludes between military campaigns, but peace never lasted long enough for vineyards to be tended.[2] In Silesia, in the fifteenth century, war precipitated an economic crisis which was exacerbated by a spell of exceptionally bad weather. Eventually, that province in what is now south-western Poland was partly depopulated, as peasants lost their lives or fled in the hope of starting over elsewhere.[3] Similarly, there is evidence that many of the colonial lords in late thirteenth-century Ireland had difficulty recruiting agricultural labour to work on their manors; and this often seems to have been because of the warfare, or the threat of warfare, with the native Irish.[4]

The March of Wales had one of the greatest castle densities of Europe. It was argued in the previous chapter that this was very largely due to its character as a military borderland in the late eleventh, twelfth and thirteenth centuries. If there is one part of the Latin west which can be expected to show the effects of long-lasting exposure to high medieval warfare on a region's economy, then the March is it. Yet this was not the whole story. The explosive rate at which castles were built show how frequently warfare erupted in the Welsh borders and in the south of Wales. But despite this, by the thirteenth century, the March was anything but an economic wasteland. In 1095, the Normans, in retribution for the coordinated Welsh attacks on their castles, 'ravaged Gower and Cydweli and Ystrad Tywi', as has been seen. The chronicler goes on to add 'and the lands remained waste'.[5] Yet despite this and later ravagings, those lands did not remain 'waste' indefinitely. By the early fourteenth century, these were among the richest Marcher lordships in Wales. The lordship of Gower was worth £300 a year to its lord in 1316; Cydweli was valued at £333 in 1331.[6]

Part of the explanation for this apparent paradox lies in wider European history. The period during which the March of Wales was created, that between the late eleventh and late thirteenth centuries, falls squarely within the high, or central, Middle Ages. This was hardly an age of peace. Much of European society was militarized and frequently at war, as is perhaps most dramatically shown by the crusades and by the reconquest of the Iberian peninsula. Between 1100 and 1300, there were many lands of war in Europe and around the Mediterranean to rival the March of Wales. One of the four horsemen of the apocalypse remained very much on the rampage. But it cannot be denied that the high Middle Ages were relatively free from famine and from pestilence – at least by medieval standards. On a long-term view, this period in European history was sandwiched between two truly cataclysmic episodes. The first was marked by the devastating raids of Vikings, Saracens and Hungarians which took place during the eighth, ninth and tenth centuries. The second began shortly after 1300. In the fourteenth century, populations everywhere in Europe were decimated by catastrophic hunger crises and a series of plague pandemics which was ushered in by the Black Death of 1348–50. In between these two nadirs there occurred an age of remarkable economic growth.[7] Even the weather appears to have been exceptionally warm during the high Middle Ages.

True, the annalists of the *Anglo-Saxon Chronicle* painted a dire picture of British weather *c.*1000–1150, frequently complaining about cold, damp and resulting crop losses.[8] But in any case, a more clement climate and a reprieve from famine and pestilence were certainly not the only explanation for economic development in the March. Rather, the political and military history of the March of Wales, the battles, campaigns and conquests by which the lordships were carved out, and the economic history of the March are two sides of the same coin. The Marcher lords did not spend generations fighting to gain control over Welsh lands purely for the military thrill. In many cases that assuredly was part of the motivation. But even for the Mortimer lords of Wigmore, military glory and family honour were not everything. The chronicle of Wigmore priory, a house of Augustinian canons established by the Mortimers in the twelfth century, gratefully records the gift of a field next to the abbey called 'Mortimer's Treasure', a name hinting at what arable land was worth to the Mortimers.[9] To give another example, in a rather wistful passage, Gerald of Wales describes the castle where he was born, Manorbier in Pembrokeshire, and in so doing draws a picture of a late twelfth-century seignorial residence.

> Only about three miles from Pembroke Castle is the fortified mansion known as Manorbier ... There the house stands, visible from afar because of its turrets and crenellations ... just beneath the walls, there is an excellent fish-pond, well constructed and remarkable for its deep waters. On the same side there is a most attractive orchard, shut in between the fish-pond and a grove of trees, with ... hazel-nut trees which grow to a great height ... [B]etween the castle, if I may call it such, and the church, a stream of water which never fails winds its way along a valley ... It runs down from a large lake, and there is a water-mill on its bank. To the west ... the castle looks out to the Irish Sea ... Boats on their way to Ireland from almost any part of Britain scud by before the east wind ... This is a region rich in wheat, with fish from the sea and plenty of wine for sale.[10]

The way in which Gerald chose to express his love of his birthplace and the value the Mortimers placed on their cornfields bespeak the same outlook. The Marcher lords may have been military men. But ultimately the aim in creating a Marcher lordship was to gain control over an economically valuable territory in order to exploit it.

The potential for gain was often considerable. So was the challenge facing the lords: nothing less was required of them than to create the conditions in which a medieval regional economy might thrive. To give an example of the variety of economic life in a twelfth-century Marcher lordship, it is worth quoting another evocative passage from Gerald of Wales. The people of Brecon lordship, he claims, were wont to perform a bizarre ritual in order to atone for working on a Sunday. He maintains it traditionally took place on the feast-day of St Eluned:

> You can see young men and maidens, some in the church itself, some in the churchyard and others in the dance which threads its way round the graves. They sing traditional songs, all of a sudden they collapse on the ground, and then those who, until now, have followed their leader peacefully as if in a trance, leap in the air as if seized by frenzy. In full view of the crowds they mime with their hands and feet whatever work they have done contrary to the commandment on sabbath days. You can see one man putting his hand

to an [imaginary] plough, another goading on his oxen with a stick ... This man is imitating a cobbler at his bench, that man over there is miming a tanner at his work. Here you see a girl pretending that she has a distaff in her hand, drawing out the thread with her hands, stretching it at arm's length, and then winding it back onto the spindle; another, as she trips along, fits the woof to the warp; a third tosses her shuttle ... and ... seems for all the world to be weaving cloth from the thread which she has prepared.[11]

It is difficult to imagine why Gerald would have made something like this up. He knew Brecon well: he was archdeacon there from about 1175 until 1203. He could have been a regular onlooker. For present purposes, the obvious point to be noted is that, to Gerald and his intended audience, the custom was extraordinary and worth recording because the trades were being mimed in a sort of mass ritual. The trades themselves were among the most commonplace occupations for the working populace of the marches – for the men, those of ploughman, cowherd, cobbler and tanner, for the women, spinning wool and weaving cloth. It was flourishing lordships like Brecon (Gerald also notes the abundance of grain there)[12] that ultimately made the fight worthwhile for the Marcher lords.

For the first Norman conquerors, a lordship like later twelfth-century Brecon was still a distant prospect. After 1066, military concerns generally outweighed economic considerations. For instance, in the building of Hen Domen Montgomery castle, part of an adjacent arable field was destroyed.[13] We only know this because it is one of the results yielded by decades of exceptionally thorough archaeological excavations. Hen Domen was probably the first castle built by the earl of Shrewsbury beyond Offa's Dyke. In strategic terms, it was crucial. It guarded a nearby ford in the river Severn, and it commanded a full view of that river's upper valley, which leads westwards into Wales. Domesday Book records that Earl Roger had but four ploughlands in demesne here in 1086.[14] It must have been a wrench to destroy any of the local arable, but the lord of Montgomery faced a stark choice, and made his decision as a military commander rather than an entrepreneur. Yet even in the conditions prevailing on the Welsh borders in the late eleventh century, it would appear that, if they set their minds to it, the Normans might improve the profitability of their estates considerably within the space of a generation or so. The manor of Clun, which Roger de Montgomery had bestowed on one Picot de Sai, had been worth 'before 1066 £25; later £3; now, of what Picot has, £6 5s; of what the knights have, £4 less 5s'.[15] Similarly, within the space of the twenty years between 1066 and 1086, the manor of Worthen, the chief estate of Roger Corbet, ancestor of the lords of Caus, had plummeted from £10 to 10 shillings before rising back up to £5 for Roger and £4 10s for his knights.[16]

Population, its size and trend of development, is fundamental to any social and economic history. However, our evidence for both is largely impressionistic when it comes to medieval Wales.[17] Gerald of Wales thought that levying Peter's Pence on all the households in Wales would yield 200 marks. A mark was two-thirds of a pound, and a pound contained 240 pence. Thus, Gerald was estimating a total 32,000 Welsh households.[18] Even if this is accepted, the trouble is knowing how large the households might, on average, have been, in later twelfth-century Wales. The numbers of five per household, and 160,000 in total, have been suggested.[19] No one has yet found a way of actually checking such a figure for medieval Wales. The same is true for the March. Even the surveys and extents which were made of several of the Marcher lordships serve to tantalize rather than enlighten the historical demographer. They were drawn up to record the dues owed to the lords rather than to count tenants. For the later thirteenth century, we have thirteen parchment rolls recording the assessments made in 1292 for Edward I's first tax on Wales. On the basis of these, it has been proposed, with great circumspection, that perhaps the population of native Wales and of the March together lay in the region of 300,000.[20]

The sources and archaeological evidence do generally convey the strong impression that the population of Wales was growing, possibly quite fast, just as it was in Britain and in Continental Europe. Gerald himself observed that, since the days of the first Norman invaders, the population of Wales had increased.[21] The boom which the Cistercian order enjoyed after 1140 in Wales proper may indicate a growing population.[22] It is also probably safe to say that, during the twelfth and thirteenth centuries, population in the March was on the rise too, despite the impact of Marcher warfare. By the later twelfth century, it was apparently possible to recruit from the southern March a fair share of the manpower needed to colonize whole Irish kingdoms, a strategy notably put into practice by William the Marshal.[23] Relocation to Ireland can hardly have been contemplated by those wishing to escape life in a military borderland. It may be that some of the knights and peasants who crossed the Irish Sea from the Welsh March were being crowded out because arable land was already becoming scarce in their homeland.[24] Some of them may have been bond villeins who were enticed by the prospect of becoming free peasants (by the fourteenth century, most free tenants on Irish manors were of English or Welsh origin).[25] The evidence for emigration from the March to Ireland in the later twelfth century certainly does not point to a scarce population.

While caution is needed in view of the gaps in our knowledge, it does not then seem as if the March lagged behind native Wales in terms of population growth because of the impact of warfare. What does seem highly probable, however, is that population growth in the March was driven to a far greater extent by immigration, from England and further afield, than was the case in Wales.[26] At first the arrival of immigrants may have had a neutral or even negative impact on population density. According to the Welsh chronicles, the settlement of Flemings, which proceeded by Henry I's permission, entailed the removal of the entire local populace.[27] On the other hand, when Gilbert fitz Richard de Clare brought English settlers to Ceredigion in the first half of the twelfth century, it was said to be 'to fill the land, which before that was almost completely empty from a scarcity of people'.[28] This is perhaps not entirely plausible, but not easy to corroborate from other sources. A point of comparison, however, is provided by the English incursions into Ireland in the 1160s and 1170s. Here, it seems clear that peasant cultivators were indeed displaced. The Treaty of Windsor (1175) between Henry II and Ruaidrí Ua Conchobair (Rory O'Connor), the high-king of Ireland, encouraged their return; indeed, it stipulated that Irishmen who had fled could be forced to come back.[29] Another point of comparison is later, but closer to home. After 1282, in the newly created Marcher lordships in north Wales, significant settlement by English peasants took place. This appears to have been closely supervised by the Marcher lords, and completed within a matter of twenty years.[30]

Presumably the scale and tempo of immigration into the March between 1067 and 1282 was partly determined by growing pressure on land in England, from where most immigrants came. It may also be that settlers tended to arrive at times when Marcher hostilities abated somewhat, such as the reign of Henry I (1100–35), or in the later twelfth and early thirteenth centuries. The Flemings who settled in Dyfed certainly began doing so in 1107–10, at the express invitation of the English king and no doubt having received some guarantees of military support.[31] One would surmise, however, that a certain amount of enticement was also often required to persuade settlers to take the chance of starting a new life in the militarily volatile Marcher lordships.

When the threat and reality of warfare grew more acute, Marcher lords may have had to offer better terms to potential immigrants. One very effective way of doing so was to establish a borough; and there was certainly no lack of new towns in the early March. A burgage plot offered the prospect of legally free personal status in return for a minimal rent. In twelfth-century Cardiff, one burgage plot could be had for only 12 pence due annually to the lord, the earl of Gloucester.[32] Burgesses could sell or let out their plots so long as the services were still performed; and the burgage plots were heritable. Burgesses were free not to use their lord's mill, to full and dye cloth, to sell their cattle and merchandise, brew and bake. If a burgess was summoned to attend his lord's court but was just about to leave for a journey, he was quit on that occasion (so long as he could provide witnesses to prove he had his foot in the stirrup when summoned). The burgesses of Cardiff were also quit of most tolls at Gloucester and throughout Gloucestershire.

The prospect of starting a new life as a burgess clearly exerted a strong attraction even in the early violent days of the eleventh-century border earls. William fitz Osbern himself is known to have founded boroughs at the castles of Wigmore and of Clifford.[33] It seems almost certain that he would have followed this up with a grant of the 'liberties of Breteuil' which he had already bestowed on Hereford. By 1086, Rhuddlan's burgesses had been granted the same privileges. There were as yet only eighteen burgesses, but this was clearly thought to be just a beginning: archaeological work has shown that the earthworks of this fledgling town embraced around thirty-five acres.[34] In principle, urban liberties would presumably have exerted as great an attraction on Welshmen as on Englishmen. But in practice, Marcher towns remained bastions of Englishness while the March was taking shape. Sometime between 1288 and 1313, the townsmen in Glamorgan referred to themselves with deliberate emphasis as 'the English burgesses of the English boroughs'. At Aberafan, which was one of the very few native urban foundations in Wales, the townsmen were mainly Welsh; nevertheless, they were described as the lord's 'Englishmen' in the second half of the thirteenth century.[35] In Carmarthen, one Meilyr Fychan owned four burgages in 1268 and soon afterwards became reeve of the borough; but the overwhelming majority of townspeople there at the time had English names.[36] It was notably the older foundations, such as Swansea and Brecon, which demonstrably remained mainly English even in the later medieval period, when newer boroughs more commonly had a mixed Anglo-Welsh population.[37]

The Normans reintroduced towns to Wales for the first time since Roman days.[38] The new towns in the March perhaps remained the strongest magnets for immigrants in the twelfth and thirteenth centuries. But they were by no means the only ones. As in other parts of high medieval Europe, so in the March lords often lacked not land but the labour to work it.[39] As a result, Marcher peasants had to expect to live and work on a manor belonging to a lord; that is, in return for grants of land they would owe rents and services. But the benefits they received in return often compared very favourably indeed with the conditions prevailing on English manors. For the March, the earliest evidence we have to illustrate this in any detail is the 1307 survey of a small manor belonging to the lady Joan de Ralegh, Michaelston-le-Pit, just to the south of Cardiff. In 1307, Seliman Day, a customary tenant on the manor of Michaelston, held of his lady one messuage, or dwelling, eleven acres of land and half an acre of meadow. For this he owed the following services: one day's ploughing for corn and one for oats; two days' harrowing; supplying one man with a horse to work with three of the other customary tenants' horses; harrowing before the sowing of the oats, each horse being allowed a handful of oats daily; mowing two acres of meadow without his lady's providing food; finding one man throughout haymaking; one to make haystacks whenever necessary, one to weed the lady's corn each week, and one to reap the corn on the lady's demesne for two days each week from the beginning of the harvest until Michaelmas. Seliman also had to help to fill the mill pond, to repair the mill and to build houses. Further, he owed carrying services, his heirs owed the best animal of his herd when he died, and he was charged a fine if his daughter married outside the lady's fee. Altogether, this was valued at 5 shillings.[40] Compared to the free tenants on Michaelston manor, admittedly, Seliman was not to be envied. One of them, John Conan, held nineteen acres and a half at a place called, unflatteringly, 'le Hole', and owed all of 2 shillings at the feast of St Andrew and two at St Michael's; he also did suit at the lady's court twice a year. After his death, his heirs owed double the amount of his rent as a heriot. On the other hand, Seliman was much better off than bondmen or villeins on most manors in England, on which unrest simmered and indeed erupted on several occasions long before the Peasants' Revolt of 1381.[41]

Thus, it is probable that many of the immigrants were lured with offers of land to be held on favourable terms. It may be that on many manorial estates in the March, the unfree tenants, those with least rights and owing the heaviest rents and services, tended to be the Welsh. This was certainly the case on the lordships established after 1283.[42] For the older manors, we generally only have late evidence; but this kind of evidence can, with circumspection, be used to illuminate earlier periods. Thus, we know that, in sixteenth-century Glamorgan, some of the free tenants held by military tenure; but that there was also a group of thirty-three freemen holding 350 acres of land in socage tenure. These legal and customary distinctions could really only have originated many centuries earlier. For one thing, socage tenure was most common in northern and eastern England, the former Danelaw. More pertinently, we also know that in the late thirteenth century there was in that part of Glamorgan a group of free tenants with small parcels of land, most of them with English names. It is definitely a good bet that tenants like these, and indeed possibly their twelfth-century predecessors, already held by socage. More research is needed to substantiate this further.[43] But since socage tenure entailed particularly low rents and services, it is tempting to see here evidence of a deal struck with English immigrants to the March at a time when Glamorgan was still liable to come under Welsh attack.

Monks formed a numerically smaller element among the immigrants who ventured into the March in this period.[44] Lords had a panoply of motives in establishing religious houses in their lordships. Naturally, they hoped to save their souls and those of their relatives, and a number of them took a monk's habit *in extremis* or, in any case, insisted on being buried in their family foundations. But the conditions of the March also played a role. It has been suggested that the Cistercian abbey of Margam in Glamorgan was partly established to stem the tide of Welsh resettlement which had begun to advance during Stephen's reign. A wide variety of different orders were represented in the March, since many of the monastic establishments there were daughter houses of abbeys close to the home castles of the Marcher lords in question. The pioneering monastic communities in the March therefore often came from mother houses in Normandy.

Whatever persuaded immigrants to settle in the March, there is every indication that there were powerful motivating forces at work. English place-names, and even field-names, abound in sources from the twelfth- and thirteenth-century March.[45] There are about 350 place-names ending in -*ton* in modern Wales; hardly any appear in our sources before *c.*1200, and almost all are located in the Marcher lordships, for instance within the pre-1974 boundaries of Pembrokeshire (155), in Glamorgan (74), in Monmouthshire (35) and in Flintshire (25).[46] Field-names may testify to the density of peasant settlement in places such as lowland Glamorgan, where in 1307 we find 'Grybbellond', 'Robyneslond',

'Ferlyngmede', 'Wyllecockescrofte', 'la Calfecrofte', and descriptions such as 'under The house' and 'atte breche'.[47] In Gower, English peasant settlement had evidently made fairly substantial progress by the beginning of the thirteenth century. Thus, in 1217, Rhys Gryg is recorded as having driven the English from the peninsula, settling Welshmen in their place.[48] In thinking of the March between 1067 and 1283 as a military borderland, we must bear in mind the apparently paradoxical fact that it was, at the same time, a destination for immigrants from England and even further abroad.

The question is how much, as a result of immigration, the March came to differ from native Wales in terms of social and economic development and organization. By the time Gerald of Wales wrote, there was certainly the perception that there existed a deep gulf in these respects.[49] Gerald was convinced that the Welsh were short on arable produce. A king wishing to conquer Wales, he muses at one point, should opt for a winter campaign. This would allow him effectively to lay siege to the entire country first. To do so, he needed to take care to cut off the trade in certain goods from England: in the autumn, besides garrisoning and provisioning castles to fortify

> not only the marches but certain carefully chosen localities in the interior ... he must make every effort to stop the Welsh buying the stocks of cloth, salt and corn which they usually import from England. Ships manned with picked troops must patrol the coast, to make sure that these goods are not brought by water across the Irish Sea or the Severn Sea ...[50]

Gerald's view of Welsh society as essentially pastoral should not be considered in isolation from what ecclesiastics like him were writing about the Scots, the Irish and indeed the pagan Slavs of eastern Europe.[51] He himself reveals that Anglesey was called *Môn mam Cymru*, 'the Mother of Wales', because it could provide all of Gwynedd with corn 'for a long period'.[52] But in his home lordship of Pembroke, it may indeed have been rare for the Welsh to have been left with arable lands. Quite possibly, such realities underlie Gerald's sweeping statements about the Welsh in general.[53]

We certainly need to take into account an element of distortion in assessing Gerald's views. The March was as diverse in economic terms as it was with respect to geographical factors such as altitude, relief and soils. The same was true of native Wales. Nevertheless, it is fair to say that much of the March contrasted with regard to terrain and soils with much of unoccupied Wales. After all, the Norman and English incursions into Wales were not undertaken randomly. Would-be Marcher lords had clear preferences with regard to the land they targeted for occupation. It may be that in this regard they were paralleled by the Normans who settled in the north of England. There, it has been argued, Norman settlement was heaviest by far in areas suitable for the cultivation of wheat. Land which would only yield oat crops was considered second-rate. As a consequence, according to this view, the Normans' first choice of land in the north was that lying to the east of the Pennines. Cumbria was settled later, during Henry I's reign, by men who had not benefited from the first onslaught on Northumbria.[54] There is certainly reason to believe that many of the Norman and English occupiers of Welsh territory were guided by such choosiness. That this was so is of course indicated by the siting of the earliest Marcher castles. Besides strategic considerations, this was clearly determined by the wish to control comparatively level lowlands with fertile soils such as coastal Glamorgan, Gower, Pembrokeshire and Ceredigion. On the other hand, the immigrants to Wales were not fixated on corn to the exclusion of all else. By the mid-twelfth century, Maurice de Londres had 'a great flock of sheep' in his lordship of Cydweli, according to Gerald of Wales.[55] He also noted that by around the same time, many of the Flemings of south Wales were sheep-farmers.[56]

Many Marcher manors were entirely new creations, established 'in the wilderness which no one had previously ploughed', as the 'township' founded by Roger Sturmy in Glamorgan apparently was.[57] English place-names containing the adjective 'new' probably originated in a similar way. A Glamorgan vill called 'Newland' is documented to as early as about 1129.[58] The first and indeed abiding task of the tenantry on these estates was assarting (from the Old French verb meaning 'to hoe'), the clearing of woodland to gain arable. In the March, the lords were colonial lords, often able to start from a blank slate. The landscape around Cardiff may serve to illustrate this. Less than a mile to the east of Cardiff castle lay the manor of Roath, which in the early 1300s was largely populated by free tenants, fifty-seven in all, holding small parcels of land 'by ancient enfeoffment'. There were only seventeen customary tenants, each holding ten or twelve acres. However, the lord had just under 300 acres of arable in demesne. Roath, it would appear, was geared towards providing dairy products for the occupants of Cardiff castle. The nearby manor of Leckwith, two miles south-west of the castle, served a completely different purpose. It was inhabited by twenty-two customary tenants who possessed twelve- or six-acre parcels of land and owed labour and carrying services throughout Glamorgan lordship.[59] Thus, in the early fourteenth century, Roath and Leckwith still bore the stamp of having been tailored to suit the needs of the lord at Cardiff.

Arguably the most distinctive feature of Marcher manors, however, was their common division into Englishries and Welshries. Ogmore, a mesne lordship in Glamorgan, in fact consisted of two detached parts, one centred on the castle in the lowlands, and one in the uplands some ten kilometres north called Glyn Ogwr, Ogmore in the Wood. The two parts were separated by another lordship, Coity. How that situation developed is still something of a mystery. But by the fifteenth century – and again the late medieval sources must reflect the earlier situation to some extent – the tenantry of the northern, upland part of Ogmore was entirely Welsh, and owed the lord only customary Welsh dues, albeit in cash rather than kind.[60] The development of many of the Welshries still needs to be reconstructed. But it illustrates particularly well the close tie between the extension of Marcher military and economic domination. The latter depended entirely on the former, particularly in the case of the remoter, Welsh-populated parts of Marcher lordships. In 1267, the *post-mortem* inquest into the possessions of John Fitzalan II resignedly stated that 'in the forest of Clun there was a large Welshry which used to be worth much to the lord both in demesne renders and in other perquisites and dues which we cannot now extend because of the disturbances wrought by the Welsh'.[61]

The interplay of the military and the economic strands in Marcher history is also evident in the towns. Not a few of the new foundations proved abortive. Some were replaced by nearby successors. Hen Domen Montgomery castle harboured burgage plots by 1201; a charter drawn up in 1215 mentions 'the town of Montgomery', which can only have referred to Hen Domen. But after 1223, New Montgomery was founded, after the first venture had been destroyed by the Welsh.[62] New Radnor, similarly, succeeded an earlier attempt at urban plantation. Cardiff, at the end of the thirteenth century, had at least 380 burgages.[63] But several of the other towns in south Wales were situated with scant consideration for economic viability. The founders of the towns of Laugharne, Llanstephan and Cydweli, say, were less concerned with establishing easily accessible market centres than with ensuring that their plantations could be resupplied from the sea if besieged. Similarly, some of the new inland boroughs – Painscastle in Elfael or Cefnllys in Maelienydd – were situated on defensible hilltop sites conspicuously lacking in any economic rationale.[64] It fits in well with this picture that some of the

Marcher burgesses owed their lords military service, as is attested for twelfth-century Swansea.⁶⁵

The March was a land of many lords and therefore of too many boroughs. As urban plantations proliferated, they entered into fierce competition with each other. Paradoxically, therefore, in the March warfare could actually ensure a town's survival, rather than bring about its ruin. In 1200, the lord of Caus received permission to hold a weekly market at his castle, and it was probably at around that time that the town of Caus began to grow up in the castle bailey. The town's position on the Long Mountain was well defensible and gave it an edge over other, more exposed settlements – such as nearby Hen Domen Montgomery. It grew steadily throughout the twelfth and thirteenth centuries. It contained twenty-eight burgage-tenements in 1274, thirty-four in 1300 and fifty-eight *c.*1349. However, the removal or the dwindling of the Welsh threat after *c.*1300 meant the town no longer derived a strategic advantage from its situation. Worse, its hilltop situation began to reduce its viability as a centre for trade, particularly as it lay between New Montgomery and Shrewsbury. These were clearly two of the reasons why the town never recovered after the onslaught of the Black Death in 1348–50. Over the subsequent centuries, it shrank gradually. The number of burgages dwindled from twenty in 1455 to ten in 1541. Today, only the castle ruins remain, although the course of one of the vanished town's streets is still visible in the fields nearby.⁶⁶ The Mortimer's urban foundation of Cefnllys was perched, as its name ('ridge-court') suggests, in a similarly elevated and inaccessible position. Its decline after 1283 was yet more rapid: as early as 1332, only twenty burgesses remained there.⁶⁷

Besides military security, the Marcher towns evidently aimed for the greatest possible economic self-sufficiency.⁶⁸ Like the true colonists they were, the earliest Marcher burgesses were keenly aware of their potentially isolated situation. As such, they were anxious to secure exclusive rights to the economic resources of their towns' hinterlands. In many of the earliest Marcher town charters, therefore, the emphasis is in fact not on urban but on agrarian privileges such as rights of pasture and common. The boundaries of the town of Cydweli, founded in 1308, extended some considerable distance beyond the actual borough settlement, so as to include a broad swathe of agricultural land around it. Many Marcher burgesses were, in terms of the work they did, fairly indistinguishable from peasants working to sustain themselves.⁶⁹ Many of the new towns, however, proved to be triumphant stories of success and magnificently lucrative enterprises for the heirs of their founders.

The March was very largely a region of secular landholders. The economic impact of the newly founded Marcher abbeys is unlikely to have been negligible; but for lack of evidence it seems scarcely possible yet to say if their economic impact was proportionally greater in the March or in Wales. It is true that there were more Cistercian abbeys in Wales proper than in the March, and it was the Cistercians, with their reforming zeal and aim to achieve economic self-sufficiency, who had the most significant economic impact on the lands they managed themselves.[70] Their economic initiative must also have provided a more general fillip to agriculture as well as to milling, mining and the production and trade of wool. However, it does seem clear that, although the Marcher Cistercian houses were fewer in number than those of Wales proper, they were, by the late thirteenth century at the latest, far wealthier. This was especially true of the abbeys in the southern Marcher lordships. When the pope imposed an ecclesiastical tax in 1292, the Glamorgan abbeys of Margam and Neath were valued at £256 and £236 gross. Grace Dieu, in Monmouth lordship, was less wealthy. But Tintern abbey, which was in Chepstow lordship, was valued at £145.[71] The Welsh Cistercian abbeys, by contrast, were among the poorest monastic houses in Britain at the time. Moreover, we do know that, in the mid-thirteenth century, the monks of Tintern 'assisted with their ploughs' in the cultivation of lands in Gwent belonging to the earl of Gloucester, 'at his request and not of any duty'.[72] Around the same time, the Cistercians of Margam were acquiring licences from various English and Welsh landowners to mine coal, lead and iron. By then, the monks of Monmouth, Tintern and Grace Dieu had a stake in the iron industry based in the Forest of Dean.[73] It seems quite possible that the Marcher Cistercians could hold their own against those in native Wales in terms of the relative economic impact they had on their surroundings.

The March has its own distinctive social and economic history as well as its own political history. The Marcher lordships were the product of warfare; but their purpose was to make possible the exploitation of local economies, and many did so successfully. The very Marcher lords who at first wrought havoc in the Welsh kingdoms also had an interest in developing their newly acquired estates. Therefore, the March offers an opportunity to study the role of landlords during the booming high Middle Ages alongside the effects of prolonged warfare.

The economic history of Wales during this period has recently been referred to as the single greatest economic transformation of Wales before the Industrial Revolution and the rise of Methodism.[74] As far as the March is concerned, one area of particular and abiding interest is the chronology, scale and impact of immigration. Between 1067 and 1283, population pressure on land in the March may have fluctuated considerably over the medium term. The later evidence of the lordships created by Edward I shows this particularly well. But much careful research is still needed, both on the period before 1066 and on the two subsequent centuries, if the impact of the March on the economic history of medieval Britain is to be fully appreciated.

Notes

[1] M. Strickland, *War and Chivalry: The Conduct and Perception of War in England and Normandy, 1066–1217* (Cambridge, 1996), ch. 10.

[2] R. Boutruche, 'The devastation of rural areas during the Hundred Years War and the agricultural recovery of France', in P. S. Lewis (ed.), *The Recovery of France in the Fifteenth Century* (New York and London, 1971), pp. 23–59.

[3] R. C. Hoffman, 'Warfare, weather and a rural economy: the duchy of Wroclaw in the mid-fifteenth century', *Viator*, 4 (1973), 273–405.

[4] K. Down, 'Colonial society and economy in the high Middle Ages', in A. Cosgrove (ed.), *A New History of Ireland*, vol. 2, *Medieval Ireland 1169–1534* (Oxford, 1987), p. 447.

[5] *Brut*, pp. 34–5.

[6] Davies, *Lordship and Society*, pp. 196–8.

[7] For a recent introduction to the social and economic history of medieval Britain cf. C. Dyer, *Making a Living in the Middle Ages: The People of Britain 850–1250* (New Haven and London, 2002).

[8] J. Thirsk (ed.), *The Agrarian History of England and Wales*, vol. 2, *1042–1350* (Cambridge, 1988), pp. 44, 722–3; E. Miller (ed.), *The Agrarian History of England and Wales*, vol. 3, *1348–1500* (Cambridge, 1991), p. 38; H. E. Hallam, 'The climate of eastern England 1250–1350', *Agricultural History Review*, 32 (1984), 124–32.

[9] 'The Anglo-Norman chronicle of Wigmore abbey', ed. J. C. Dickinson and P. T. Ricketts, *Transactions of the Woolhope Naturalists' Field Club*, 39 (1969), 442–3.

[10] Gerald of Wales, *Journey/Description*, pp. 150–1 (*Journey*, i, 12); cf. *The Autobiography of Gerald of Wales*, ed. and trans. H. E. Butler (London, 1937); D. J. C. King and J. C. Perks, 'Manorbier castle, Pembrokeshire', *Arch. Camb.*, 119 (1970), 83–118.

[11] Gerald of Wales, *Journey/Description*, pp. 92–3 (*Journey*, i, 2).

[12] Ibid.

[13] P. A. Barker and J. Lawson, 'A pre-Norman field system at Hen Domen, Montgomery', *Medieval Archaeology*, 15 (1972 for 1971), 58–72; DB 253c.

[14] DB 252.

[15] DB 258.
[16] DB 255.
[17] The same is true for Ireland: Down, 'Colonial society and economy', p. 448.
[18] *Giraldus Cambrensis, De invectionibus*, ed. W. S. Davies in *Y Cymmrodor*, 30 (1920), 138–9 (ii, 5). In Gerald's day, Peter's Pence was a papal tax levied on English households.
[19] F. G. Cowley, *The Monastic Order in South Wales, 1066–1349* (Cardiff, 1977), p. 54.
[20] K. Williams-Jones, *The Merioneth Lay Subsidy Roll, 1292–3* (Cardiff, 1976), pp. xxxv–lxvii, esp. p. lix.
[21] Gerald of Wales, *Journey/Description*, pp. 266–7 (*Description*, ii, 7); Davies, *Age of Conquest*, pp. 146–9.
[22] Cowley, *Monastic Order*, pp. 46–7, 84–6.
[23] F. X. Martin, 'John, lord of Ireland, 1185–1216', in Cosgrove (ed.), *New History of Ireland*, vol. 2, pp. 151, 155; Down, 'Colonial society and economy', p. 444.
[24] H. Pryce, 'In search of a medieval society: Deheubarth in the writings of Gerald of Wales', *WHR*, 13 (1987), 267.
[25] Down, 'Colonial society and economy', p. 456.
[26] Davies, *Age of Conquest*, pp. 97–100, 147.
[27] *Brut*, pp. 52–3 (annal for 1108); on the immigrant Flemings, cf. I. W. Rowlands, 'The making of the March: aspects of the Norman settlement in Dyfed', *Proceedings of the Battle Conference on Anglo-Norman Studies*, 3 (1981 for 1980), pp. 146–8.
[28] *Brut*, pp. 92–3 (annal for 1116).
[29] Martin, 'John, lord of Ireland', p. 151 and n. 2; Down, 'Colonial society and economy', p. 444; *Irish Historical Documents*, ed. E. Curtis and R. B. McDowell (London, 1943), no. 4, pp. 22–4, at p. 23.
[30] Davies, *Lordship and Society*, pp. 342–3.
[31] *Brut*, pp. 52–3 (annal for 1108).
[32] *Cartae*, i, no. 113, p. 93; no. 102, p. 104; D. G. Walker, 'Cardiff', in R. A. Griffiths (ed.), *Boroughs of Mediaeval Wales* (Cardiff, 1978), pp. 120–1.
[33] DB 183; Lloyd, *History of Wales*, p. 375.
[34] DB 269; H. Quinnell and M. R. Blockley, *Excavations at Rhuddlan, Clwyd, 1969–1973: Mesolithic to Medieval* (York, 1994), pp. 214–16; M. Bateson, 'The laws of Breteuil', *English Historical Review*, 15 (1900), 302–3.
[35] *Cartae*, iii, no. 811, pp. 922–3; cf. *Cartae*, iv, no. 1001, p. 1275 (dated to 1350); Davies, *Lordship and Society*, p. 325.
[36] R. A. Griffiths, 'Carmarthen', in *Boroughs of Mediaeval Wales*, p. 151.
[37] *GCH*, iii, 372–3; 'The charters of the boroughs of Brecon and Llandovery', ed. W. Rees, *BBCS*, 2 (1923–4), 253–4.
[38] R. A. Griffiths, 'Wales and the marches', in D. M. Palliser (ed.), *The Cambridge Urban History of Britain*, vol. 1 (Cambridge, 2000), pp. 681–714.
[39] R. Bartlett, *The Making of Europe: Conquest, Colonization and Cultural Change 950–1350* (London, 1993), p. 118.

[40] M. Griffiths, 'The manor in medieval Glamorgan: the estates of the de Ralegh family in the fourteenth and fifteenth centuries', *BBCS*, 32 (1985), 178, 194–5; cf. Somerset Record Office, DD/WO 47/1, ff. 13v–15r.

[41] Cf. H. E. Hallam, 'The life of the people', in Thirsk (ed.), *Agrarian History*, vol. 2, esp. pp. 845–53.

[42] Davies, *Lordship and Society*, pp. 383–4.

[43] National Library of Wales, Bute MSS. 99/6; NLW, Dinas Powys MSS. no. 111; *Cartae*, iii, pp. 713–57; J. B. Smith, 'The kingdom of Morgannwg and the Norman conquest of Glamorgan', in *GCH*, iii, pp. 19–22; M. Lieberman, 'Anglicization in high medieval Wales: the case of Glamorgan', *WHR*, 23 (2006), 1–26.

[44] Cowley, *Monastic Order*.

[45] B. G. Charles, *The Place-Names of Pembrokeshire* (Aberystwyth, 1992); G. O. Pierce, *The Place-Names of Dynas Powys Hundred* (Cardiff, 1968); idem, *Place-Names in Glamorgan* (Cardiff, 2002); cf. the maps in RCAHMW, *An Inventory of the Ancient Monuments in Glamorgan*, vol. 3, part 2, *Medieval Secular Monuments, Non-Defensive* (Cardiff, 1982), p. 10 (non-Celtic place-names before 1500, and between 1500 and 1715).

[46] Davies, *Age of Conquest*, p. 99.

[47] Griffiths, 'Estates of the de Ralegh family', p. 192.

[48] *Brut*, pp. 216–19.

[49] Pryce, 'Deheubarth', 272.

[50] Gerald of Wales, *Journey/Description*, p. 267 (*Description*, ii, 8); for a near-contemporary comment on Wales's dependence on imports see William of Newburgh, 'Historia rerum anglicarum', *Chronicles of the Reigns of Stephen, Henry II and Richard I*, ed. R. Howlett (4 vols, RS, 1884–9), i, 107.

[51] Bartlett, *Gerald of Wales*, ch. 6.

[52] Gerald of Wales, *Journey/Description*, p. 230 (*Description*, i, 6).

[53] Pryce, 'Deheubarth', 272.

[54] Kapelle, *Norman Conquest of the North*, ch. 7.

[55] Gerald, *Journey/Description*, pp. 137–8 (*Journey*, i, 9).

[56] *The Autobiography of Gerald of Wales*, ed. and trans. Butler, pp. 39–40, 43–4.

[57] *Cartae*, i, no. 152, p. 151; Davies, *Lordship and Society*, p. 345.

[58] *Cartae*, i, no. 68: grant to Neath Abbey of 'totam terram de Newland'.

[59] Smith, 'Morgannwg', pp. 19–21.

[60] Davies, *Lordship and Society*, pp. 305–6

[61] *Calendar of Inquisitions Post Mortem*, vol. 1, *Henry III* (London, 1904), no. 684; PRO/TNA C 132/35 (18), m. 3r.

[62] *Innocentii III, Romani pontificis, opera omnia*, ed. J.–P. Migne (4 vols, *Bibliotheca Patrum Latina*, 214–18, Paris, 1855), i, col. 944; *The Charters of the Abbey of Ystrad Marchell*, ed. G. C. G. Thomas (Aberystwyth, 1997), no. 25; P. A. Barker, 'Timber castles on the Welsh Border with special reference to Hen Domen, Montgomery', in *Les mondes Normands (viiie–xiie siècles)* (Caen, 1989), pp. 139, 145; Davies, *Lordship and Society*, p. 320.

[63] *Cartae*, iii, nos. 743–9. pp. 813–48, esp. 813–15; no. 743; *GCH*, iii, pp. 337, 342; Walker, 'Cardiff', p. 118.

[64] Davies, *Lordship and Society*, pp. 321, 334.
[65] *GCH*, iii, p. 362 (earliest Swansea charter, 1153–84); *Cartae*, i, no. 138, pp. 136–8.
[66] A. T. Gaydon (ed.), *A History of Shropshire*, vol. 8 (Oxford, 1968), p. 310.
[67] *Calendar of Inquisitions Post Mortem*, vol. 7, *Edward III* (London, 1909), no. 387, p. 280.
[68] Davies, *Lordship and Society*, p. 238; M. W. Beresford, *New Towns of the Middle Ages* (London and New York, 1967), pp. 219–25.
[69] Davies, *Lordship and Society*, p. 328; *A Survey of the Duchy of Lancaster Lordships in Wales, 1609–13*, ed. W. Rees (Cardiff, 1953), p. 192.
[70] D. H. Williams, *The Welsh Cistercians*, vol. 2 (Tenby, 1984); see also idem, *Atlas of Cistercian Lands in Wales* (Cardiff, 1990); D. M. Robinson, *The Cistercians in Wales: Architecture and Archaeology 1130–1540* (London, 2006); D. H. Williams, 'The exploration and excavation of Cistercian sites in Wales', *Arch. Camb.*, 144 (1997 for 1995), 1–25.
[71] *Taxatio ecclesiastica Angliae et Walliae auctoritate P. Nicholai IV. circa A. D. 1291*, ed. T. Astle, S. Ayscough and J. Caley (London, 1802), pp. 282–4.
[72] *Calendar of Charter Rolls*, vol. 3 (London, 1908), pp. 103–4.
[73] Cowley, *Monastic Order*, p. 54; *Cartae*, ii, no. 808, p. 564 (*c.*1249); no. 566, p. 592; no. 579, p. 605 (1253).
[74] Davies, *Age of Conquest*, p. 111.

4

The Frontier of Peoples, 1067–1300

It was during the medieval period that people in Britain began to be identified as Welsh, English or Scottish. That simple statement is incontrovertible. However, it barely scratches the surface of developments which spanned centuries, which interwove with each other and for which the sources are fascinating, but few. The various Germanic peoples who settled in Britain from the late fourth century onwards, the Angles, Saxons and Jutes, were referred to collectively as the *gens Anglorum*, the 'English people' by the Venerable Bede (d.735).[1] Shortly before 900, King Alfred called them *Angelcynn*.[2] Welshmen writing in Latin were still referring to themselves simply as 'British' in the early twelfth century, as they had done since at least the ninth. At the same time, those writing in Welsh used *Cymry* to refer to the inhabitants of Wales as well as of the British kingdom of Strathclyde or Cumbria. Welsh *Cymry*, of course, survived. By 1150, however, the Latin *Britones* or *Brittanni* had been jettisoned in favour of *Walenses* (though Gerald of Wales preferred *Cambria* and *Cambrenses* to *Wallia* and *Walenses*, observing, rightly, that the latter were derived from the English adjective *wealh*, meaning 'foreign').[3] As for the Scots, Latin *Scoti* was used to refer to the Irish who began settling in Argyll in around the year 500, but this term for a long time also designated the Irish in general. The issue was further complicated by rival perceptions about the location and extent of the territory called in Gaelic *Alba*, in Latin *Scotia* or *Albania*. Indeed, it was not even certain whether these were geographical or political terms, that is, whether they referred to a geographical entity or to a kingdom. Dauvit Broun has argued that it was not until the thirteenth century that the Scots were understood, by all the authors of our surviving written sources, to be the inhabitants of the kingdom of Scotland.[4]

The March of Wales is particularly relevant to the medieval history of two of these identities, those of the Welsh and of the English. The March was taking shape at the very time when the shift from 'British' to 'Welsh' occurred. And it was during the late eleventh and twelfth centuries that the English identity survived and indeed triumphantly reasserted itself, even though the Anglo-Saxon aristocracy had mostly lost their lives or in any case their possessions after 1066.[5] Thus, the Normans spread through England into Wales at a time when 'ethnic' identities were very much an issue. One excellent illustration of this is the usage of the Welsh annals, which generally refer to the Marchers as 'Frenchmen' throughout the twelfth and into the thirteenth centuries, but also occasionally mention 'Normans'.[6] 'Saxons', that is, 'Englishmen' occur throughout the period covered by the Welsh chronicles. Before 1066, that term of course refers to Anglo-Saxons. Thereafter, it appears to have been used to refer to peasant settlers rather than knights for a time, but armed 'Englishmen' are frequently mentioned by the later twelfth century.[7]

The first generation of Norman settlers in England and Wales undoubtedly considered itself neither English nor British nor Welsh. They are particularly well exemplified by Roger de Montgomery, the first earl of Shrewsbury, and his numerous sons, who included Arnulf, the founder of Pembroke castle, as well as Hugh and Robert, the second and third earls of Shrewsbury. Roger and his sons considered the world to be their oyster; but they had no doubts about their identity. Roger's sons were very young men when they conducted their first raids into Wales in the 1070s; Hugh was probably still a teenager. But they had all been born in Normandy, and though they cut their military teeth in Wales they often returned to their homeland and also ventured much further abroad. Only Hugh was killed in Wales; his brothers died in England, in Normandy, in France, and, indeed, at Antioch, on the First Crusade. Their boundless ambition and ruthlessness was not just characteristic of the Normans. It was typical of much of the high medieval northern French warrior class.[8] But it is fair to say that Roger de Montgomery and his sons remained Normans at heart all their life. The earl himself, in the early 1080s, had himself described as a 'Norman born of Normans'.[9] Almost certainly, such sentiments were shared by the overwhelming majority of the first Normans to arrive in Britain after 1066.[10]

But things undeniably grew far more ambiguous once the second generation started being born. The birthplace of the future Henry I of England (1068/9–1135), the youngest son of William the Conqueror, was in England, possibly at Selby. Henry I died in Normandy, but his body was returned to England, to be buried in the abbey at Reading.[11] During the twelfth century the descendants of the Normans and other Continental immigrants to England appear to have forsaken their roots, embracing an English identity. Scholars disagree about when exactly this happened. But by the late 1170s, the author of a treatise on the English exchequer could write: 'nowadays, when English and Normans live closely together and marry and give in marriage to each other, the nations are so mixed that it can scarcely be decided (I mean in the case of freemen) who is of English birth and who of Norman'.[12]

Whether this was true of the descendants of the Normans who had settled in Wales is a different question. Take Gerald of Wales. In the late 1180s, in his earliest surviving major work, *The History and Topography of Ireland*, Gerald identified with the English, referring to them as 'our own English people'.[13] In *c.*1191, he declared that with the help of his kinsmen, the descendants of Gerald of Windsor and of Nest, 'the sea-coast of South Wales was held secure by the English'.[14] Soon afterwards, however, embittered by his unsuccessful bid to succeed to the bishopric of St David's, he observed:

> Although I am by descent three-quarters English and Norman, a hostile people assumes that I am totally corrupted by the fourth part of my heritage ... Even though my upbringing (*morum institutio*) and association (*conversatio*) were among the English, my descent and family connections (*natio* and *cognatio*) were in Wales ... Both peoples regard me as a stranger ... one suspects me, the other hates me.[15]

By the early 1200s, a man who had professed to be of the English people twenty years earlier could write: 'The English are the most worthless of all peoples under heaven'.[16] Whether or not Gerald was right in believing that his mixed ancestry had limited his career options, his ethnicity was an issue of consuming importance to him. He lived in a world in which he was often made to feel an outsider.

It seems unlikely that he was alone in this. There was no insurmountable barrier to marriage, or in any case relationships, between Norman, English and Welsh men and women. To many of the first Marcher lords marriage offered an admirable opportunity to establish themselves more securely in their new environment. Gerald of Wales, himself the product of a cross-cultural marriage, made no bones about this. After relating how his grandfather, Gerald of Windsor, had cunningly defended Pembroke castle against the Welsh, he adds: 'The next thing Gerald did was to marry Nest the sister of Gruffydd, Prince of South Wales, with the object of giving himself and his troops a firmer foothold in the country.'[17] As a tool of diplomacy, intermarriage with the Normans and the English also had its attractions for the Welsh rulers. In 1175 Dafydd ab Owain Gwynedd, king of Gwynedd, married Emma of Anjou, a half-sister of Henry II's, 'thinking', according to the Welsh chronicles, 'that he would be able to have his territory in peace and quiet for that reason.'[18] The Mortimers, by the later thirteenth century, had intermarried with the dynasty of Gwynedd. One progeny of this marital union, Roger Mortimer III (d. 1282), was the first cousin of Llywelyn ap Gruffudd. It is, of course, a moot point whether this meant that Roger would have thought of himself as Welsh at all. But it is certainly a possibility. Many crises of identity like those experienced by Gerald of Wales may have been precipitated during the period *c.* 1067–1300.

None of Gerald's fellow Marchers left the explicit autobiographical statements which allow us to follow their trials and tribulations. However, Gerald's writings show him to have been acutely sensitive to the fact that there were others who found themselves in a situation comparable to his. In 1189, he penned his account of the conquests which had been made in Ireland since 1167 by knights from the March and from England, and in which a number of his southern Marcher kinsmen had played a leading role. Stylized speeches are a favourite rhetorical device in this work. One of them is given the dramatic setting of a debate among the invaders on the brink of a battle with the Irish. In this debate, Gerald has his uncle, Maurice FitzGerald, declare: 'What then are we waiting for? Surely we do not look to our own people for succour? We are now constrained in our actions by this circumstance, that just as we are English as far as the Irish are concerned, likewise to the English we are Irish ...'[19] We may wonder how commonly the inhabitants of the Welsh March might have perceived themselves to be 'Welsh to the English, and English to the Welsh'.

We are, it is true, faced with the absence of explicit personal statements. But one might take the view that ethnic identities and cultural affiliations, including Gerald's, were a matter of objective traits as well as subjective views. If this is accepted, then it follows that much is revealed in objective traits, such as language, laws or customs, about the ethnic identities of the Marchers. In defence of this line of argument, objective traits clearly bore on perceptions of ethnic identities in medieval Britain and Ireland. Bernard, the first Norman bishop of St David's (1115–48), expressed the view that the Welsh were 'entirely different in nation, language, laws and habits, judgements and customs'.[20] In 1297, the parliament in Dublin proclaimed that 'Englishmen, as if degenerate, wear Irish clothing and, having their heads half-shaved, grow their hair long at the back of the head and call it a *cúlan*, conforming to the Irish both in dress and appearance.'[21] Widespread degeneracy, in the sense of the loss of distinguishing features by the descendants of the English colonists, would appear to have been a fairly recent phenomenon in Ireland at the time.[22] And it was perceived to be a matter of external features such as clothing, hairstyle and dress.

No such legislation against ethnic 'degeneracy' relating specifically to Wales survives. True, in the March, the king of England did not normally legislate at all. It is possible that there was less acculturation and cultural assimilation between the Normans and the English on the one hand and the Welsh on the other. But this in itself would call for an explanation. Compared to Scotland, the Normans got off to a very different start in Wales. In Wales, the Normans arrived as conquerors; in Scotland, they were invited in by the native king. It remained to be seen, however, what longer-term effect this would have on cultural assimilation and on self-perceptions. In an age when the fashion was for 'universal' rather than local saints, the barons and knights of Norman descent who had made their home in south Wales adopted St David as their patron and his name as their battle-cry.[23] Moreover, even if Gerald's perceptions of the Welsh were widespread among Marcher society in his day, what happened to perceptions of the Welsh in the thirteenth century has not yet been studied in depth.[24]

Names did not appear in the Irish legislation of 1297. However, they are a part of a person's identity. In medieval Britain, they could act as badges in ethnic as well as personal terms.[25] Names in the March of Wales sometimes hint at identities just as ambiguous as those of Gerald of Wales. Around 1100, Nest, a granddaughter of Gruffudd ap Llywelyn of Gwynedd, was given the French name of Agnes after she married Bernard de Neufmarché, the Norman who first seized the Welsh kingdom of Brycheiniog.[26] One of her children (she later denied that Bernard was the father) was a son who received the French name Mahel. At around the same time, Cadwgan ap Bleddyn, a scion of the dynasty of Powys, had two sons by a daughter of Picot de Sai, the first Norman lord of Clun. The names chosen for the sons illustrate their mixed descent: the choice of Owain for one emphasized the Welsh side of the family, but the other son was named Henry, remarkably so, given that this was what the king of England was called at the time. One of the men from the southern March who began raiding Irish kingdoms after 1167 sported the hybrid name Meilyr fitz Henry. This fitted him well: his father was Henry, an illegitimate son of Henry I of England, and his mother the Welsh princess Nest from whom Gerald of Wales, too, descended.[27]

All of these examples are of Marcher lords and ladies. But combing through the evidence of monastic charters can yield nuggets of information about free peasants as well. In Glamorgan, in the 1170s, among the tenants owing suit at one of that lordship's judicial courts for the Welsh (the 'Welsh hundred') was one Cynaethwy son of Herbert son of Godwin.[28] In terms of names, the son and grandson of Godwin, who may have been an English immigrant to south Wales, progressed through a Norman-French (Herbert) to a Welsh stage (Cynaethwy).[29] Cynaethwy, moreover, had three brothers, two with Welsh names, Bleddyn and Cynwrig, and one with the most popular Anglo-French name of the age: William. The three had probably inherited equal shares of their patrimony, as groups of Welsh kinsmen would normally have done;[30] and they owed the money-value of a Welsh food-rent to their lord at Cardiff.[31] Perhaps it is important that the descendants of Godwin were based in the lower Afan valley, at some distance from secure bases of Norman and English power such as the castles at Cardiff and Swansea. However, personal names in the March also sometimes appear to show Welshmen accepting English customs. The Welsh lords of Afan themselves, who descended from Iestyn ap Gwrgant, the last native king of Morgannwg, had by 1340, and probably rather earlier, begun to call themselves 'd'Avene' in the style of English and Marcher castellans.[32] Personal names in the March are evidence of cultural exchange and assimilation.

The March was a region which saw a considerable degree of contact between speakers of different languages. Interpreters were much in demand. Gerald of Wales and Archbishop Baldwin had need of several on their tour of Wales preaching the Third Crusade.[33] Gerald also mentions that, when Henry II was in Glamorgan in 1172, one of his servants, Philip of Marcross, had to interpret when the king encountered a local man who only spoke English.[34] In 1302, an interpreter was present when 2,000 Welshmen did fealty to the new lord of Brecon;[35] five years later, the bishop of Hereford had to preach through one in the uplands of Clun lordship, where it would appear that the tenants only knew Welsh.[36] For Pembrokeshire families such as that of Gerald of Wales, it may have been common to be able to converse in Flemish, as Gerald's brother apparently did in the late twelfth century.[37] Place-names provide tantalizing hints that in some areas, such as Archenfield or Oswestry lordship, there may have been periods lasting a generation or two when bilingualism was widespread. This may account for the literal translation of place-names from Welsh into English as in the case of Peterstow and Bridstow (from Lann Petyr and Lann San Freit); it also perhaps accounts for the one translation of an Archenfield place-name from English into Welsh (Trebumfrey from Hunfreyeston, or Humphrey's 'ton').[38]

If language may have helped to identify the March as a culturally distinctive region, law most certainly did. It was fully recognized early on that the legal status of the March was singular, indeed unique. In 1215, Magna Carta characterized the legal position in the March in perhaps the most concise way possible: 'if a dispute arises . . . it shall be settled . . . for tenements in England according to the law of England, for tenements in Wales according to the law of Wales, for tenements in the March according to the law of the March'.[39] It is true that Magna Carta's scribes were availing themselves of a convenient umbrella term, knowingly or not. Other contemporary sources generally speak not of the law, but of the 'laws and customs' of the March. Indeed, more common still are references to the law of individual lordships: 'the law and custom of the land of Brecon', say.[40] Cases brought before Marcher lords or their bailiffs were adjudicated according to local custom, as determined, above all, by the memory of the populace of individual Marcher lordships, that is to say, by juries. It was also determined by the Marcher lords themselves. This hardly made for uniformity. On the other hand, it was generally true of Marcher law that it was a real hybrid. It was so in its substance. The law of the March was an amalgam, incorporating elements both of the law of Wales and of the common law of England. What is more, it also contained elements of the justice meted out by lords of manors and baronies in the English kingdom. But Marcher law was also a hybrid with respect to procedure. Marcher lords eagerly, and from an early date, imported English common law methods, most especially the practices of commencing cases by writ and terminating them by jury.

Much of the surviving evidence for Marcher law comes from the rolls kept by the courts of individual lordships, notably Clun and Caus. However, it is fourteenth century or later. There are still many mysteries about how exactly the legal situation obtaining by $c.1300$ developed. What is clear, however, is that the creation of Marcher law is closely linked to the history of the English and Welsh identities. Medieval writers often held that peoples could be identified by their laws as well as their language and ways of life.[41] For instance, for the thirteenth-century lords of Gwynedd and of Powys, the right to settle their dispute according to Welsh law was a burning issue in the political tug-of-war with the king of England; it was also, arguably, crucial to the development of the national identity of the medieval Welsh.[42] In thirteenth-century England, the importance of the common law in determining who was considered to be English was paramount.[43] Given this link between law and ethnicity, the legal distinctiveness of the March bears directly on its cultural distinctiveness. The law administered by the many courts in the Marcher lordships served as a constant reminder that the March was a region in which two peoples intermingled. The hybrid that was Marcher law mirrored the ethnic amalgam that was Marcher society, and the two must have developed hand in hand.

The same point can be made about certain typically Marcher institutions. One 'splendidly hybrid' phenomenon was the Welsh knight's fee, a technical term inspired by the abbreviated phrases found in a number of sources from the fourteenth century such as *feoda Wallens*.[44] Most Marcher knights held their fees on the same terms as English knights. The land which they held in return for military service descended by the rules of primogeniture. They were subject to wardship and marriage, that is, their lords claimed the right to have custody of the lands of minor heirs and to dispose of their marriages and the marriages of tenants' widows. As has been seen, the English kings were owed almost no knights from the conquest lordships in Wales. But the Marcher lords established knights' fees in abundance, mostly to ensure a supply of knights capable of performing castle-guard service at their fortresses. In fact, according to Professor William Rees's remarkable maps of south Wales and the border, by the fourteenth century there were around 500 knights' fees in the Marcher lordships south of the Severn.[45] Of these 400 appear to have been 'normal', English-style knights' fees, although fifty of them were actually held by tenants with Welsh names. Iorwerth ap Rees held half a knight's fee of the Clare lords in Gwynllŵg.[46] There was also a grand total of around 100 estates which were held as Welsh knights' fees or fractions or multiples of Welsh knights' fees. Thus, in the lordship of Usk, three Welsh knights' fees were held by Iorwerth Fychan, John ap Gruffudd and others 'and their partners who render no rent but give relief, to wit, 50s for a whole fee, but their heirs shall not be in wardship nor shall the lord have the marriage of them'.[47] According to Professor Rees's maps, eighty of the Welsh knights' fees in the March were held by Welshmen, the remaining twenty or so were in the hands of tenants with English names. How exactly this situation developed, and how it would have worked in practice, is still unexplained. But the existence of Welsh knights' fees speaks volumes of the scope for cultural exchange and hybridization which existed in the twelfth- and thirteenth-century March.

Objective traits, like language, law and institutions, are just some of the potential touchstones for gauging how deep was the cultural divide between the Welsh and the foreigners in the March. Customs, in the very broad sense of norms, 'the way things are done', provide another. Indeed, the broader the concept of custom is defined, the more facets of life in the March should be considered relevant. Much as the March was a melting-pot of languages and laws, so, potentially, it was also one of customs. In the March, it is worth taking a close look at conventions in warfare. For one thing, methods of fighting certainly helped to identify peoples. Indeed, one of the Welsh chronicles remarks that Magnus, the king of Norway, attacked a much larger Scottish army 'according to the custom' of the Norsemen.[48] But behaviour on the battlefield is particularly relevant to cultural transfer in Britain after 1066. For it appears that the Norman advance into Britain was accompanied by the introduction of 'chivalrous' codes of conduct in warfare.

Thus, in the case of England, it seems clear that the Norman conquest brought about a sudden change in attitudes to the appropriate treatment of enemy combatants, civilians and prisoners of war.[49] True, the battle of Hastings itself was for survival, both for the English and the Normans, and accordingly it was fought in such a way that very large numbers were killed. But there is reason to believe that this was already the exception to a rule, at least as far as the Normans were concerned. Thus, after Hastings, William the Conqueror occasionally behaved in what might be called a chivalrous fashion. As his victorious army drew near Dover, for instance, the garrison decided to surrender. William accepted, but some of his men, 'eager for booty', nevertheless set fire to the town. William of Poitiers, the Conqueror's biographer, records that the 'duke, unwilling that those who had offered to surrender should suffer loss, gave them a recompense in money for the damage of the castle and their property; and he would have severely punished those who had started the fire if their numbers and base condition had not prevented their detection'.[50] As Matthew Strickland has argued, the incident reveals that the invading army was operating on the basis of certain conventions regarding conduct in war. The Norman duke clearly considered it an outrage that besieged townsmen in the process of surrendering should come to harm; while those who set the fires were apparently hoping to prevent a capitulation, on the principle that a town or castle which had refused to surrender was fair game and could be looted.[51] Such principles, historians have recently argued, were part of a wider code of war which was entirely new to England. Before 1066, glory was to be won by dying in combat; battles between Vikings and Anglo-Saxons often ended in massacre, or in captives being sold into slavery. In the wake of the Norman conquest and of the large-scale destruction of the old Anglo-Saxon aristocracy, it became far more common in England to take prisoners in order to ransom them. True, this convention applied only to aristocrats, and the outlook of defeated infantrymen or mercenaries generally remained grim. But there is a very strong case for seeing 1066 as a sea change in conventions of warfare in England.

These conventions were introduced into England suddenly, as a direct result of conquest. In Scotland, they soon began to make headway too. Here, however, the main agents of change were the kings of Scots themselves. David I came to the throne in 1124 after growing up in exile, as a member of the household of the future Henry I of England. He was familiar with the world of Norman and English courts of the early twelfth century. It would also appear that he had been indoctrinated there with the new ideals of honour and conduct in battle. In 1138, as a token of his respect for their fortitude in surviving a particularly prolonged siege, he not only allowed the garrison of Wark to depart free and to keep their weapons; he also presented them with horses to replace the ones they had been forced to eat.[52] It is true that he also participated in the custom by which the Scots army shared out by lot those enslaved during a raid in England, along with the rest of the plunder. But he set free those allotted to him, an example followed by a number of his men.[53]

There is every reason to believe that in the March of Wales the situation was different again. In the eyes of twelfth-century observers, warfare was certainly conducted very differently in the March than in England. Something of a clash of cultures was perceived to be in progress. Gerald of Wales himself put it most eloquently and explicitly:

> In my opinion the Welsh marches would have been better controlled under the English occupation if their kings, in governing these regions and in repelling the attacks of a hostile people, had from the beginning taken the advice of the marcher lords, and used their tactics, instead of those of the Angevins and the Normans ... [Troops] who have lived all their lives in the marches will be by far the most suitable, for they have had long practice in waging war in local conditions. They are bold, speedily deployed and experienced in all that they do. As military circumstances dictate, they ride well and they advance quickly on foot ... [French and English troops] are used to fighting on the level, whereas here the terrain is rough; their battles take place in the open fields, but here the country is heavily wooded; with them the army is an honourable profession but with us it is a matter of dire necessity; their victories are won by stubborn resistance, ours by constant

movement; they take prisoners, we cut off their heads; they ransom their captives, but we massacre them.[54]

This remarkable passage shows Gerald to have been aware that there were conventions which guided knights on the battlefields of France and England. It is also striking that he focuses on the March as an arena of particularly brutal warfare. As ever, it should be stressed that Gerald's point of view was partisan.[55] Nevertheless, although there is insufficient evidence to be sure, on balance it seems probable that Norman 'chivalrous' conduct in war was alien to Wales, just as it had been alien to England. The bloodfeud was particularly well-entrenched and had a firm place within the framework of Welsh law and custom.[56] Gerald of Wales alludes darkly to atrocities committed by feuding Welshmen in the lordship of Brecon. On his journey through Wales, he met at least one Welshman who was reluctant to join the Third Crusade before he had taken vengeance for the killing of his lord, Owain ap Madog of Powys.[57] Welsh family vendettas could be extremely bloody.[58] In the pithy phrase of the Welsh annal for 1111, the members of the ruling dynasty of Powys were, in the early twelfth century, 'all of them slaying one another'.[59] Welsh rulers had to live with the threat and reality of bloodshed and mutilation. For this reason alone, it is entirely plausible that the Normans who sought to occupy their territory could expect little in the way of 'chivalrous' treatment if they were defeated. There is also the obvious consideration that rules for laying siege to castles, say, were as new to eleventh- and twelfth-century Wales as the castles themselves. In a country where coinage was not yet in widespread use, moreover, the ransoming of prisoners of war is not as likely to have been a well-established norm. It should be also be noted that in England and France, the new 'chivalrous' rules were often ignored when they conflicted too strongly with strategic considerations.[60] For the lords of the March, as Gerald rightly observed, what was at stake was always livelihood and often survival. In any case, in the cross-cultural warfare which was waged in the nascent March, there was ample scope for misunderstandings, and the mutual trust needed to uphold 'chivalrous' conventions was particularly difficult to build. Thus, there are several reasons why it might be thought that, early on, warfare in the March entailed unusually high risks to life and limb.

It is perhaps unsurprising, then, that the historical record for the late eleventh and twelfth centuries tells a decidedly unchivalrous tale. According to Orderic Vitalis, Robert of Rhuddlan slaved in north Wales.[61] The garrisons of captured castles seem, in general, not to have had the option of surrendering to save their lives. In 1094, indeed, Welsh tactics would appear to have been specifically to decimate castellans. In the words of the chronicler, 'they destroyed the [Norman] castles in Gwynedd and devised plunderings and slaughters against them'.[62] In 1116, Gruffudd ap Rhys ap Tewdwr and a band of young 'hotheads' embarked on a mission to burn as many of the Norman castles in south Wales as possible.[63] In 1167 a joint Anglo-Welsh force destroyed the Welsh castle of Caereinion and slew its garrison.[64] Apart from sieges, too, the stakes in Marcher warfare were high. The Norman lord of Ceredigion, Richard de Clare, and his retinue was killed in an ambush by Iorwerth of Caerleon in 1136.[65] Sixty years later, the Lord Rhys, in a skirmish against Roger Mortimer of Wigmore, treated his enemies 'vilely, although manfully, so that the Marchers greatly lamented the exceeding great slaughter of their men'.[66] That the slain were noblemen, at least from Mortimer's point of view, is suggested by his grant to Cwmhir abbey, made in 1199, for the souls of his men and of 'those who died in the conquest of Maelienydd'.[67]

By the thirteenth century, however, it is perhaps more difficult to be certain that slaughter or enslavement of enemies remained the universally accepted *norm* in the March. For one thing, we need to consider the state of the evidence. It may be that massacres were more likely to be noted in the English and Welsh chronicles because they were unusual, perhaps even exceptional. As vivid and detailed as our sources are, there is often little way of knowing what they left out. There is also positive evidence of restraint, even in Marcher warfare. Garrisons and townsmen sometimes managed to avert the worst by paying ransoms to besieging Welsh armies. In 1217, the townsmen of Brecon persuaded Llywelyn ab Iorwerth to lift his siege by promising to pay him 100 marks; the men of Haverford struck a similar deal in the same year.[68]

Gerald himself provides reason to believe that the contrast between warfare in the March and England may have grown less stark as time passed. In another of his conspicuously astute observations, he notes: 'The Welsh have gradually learnt from the English and the Normans how to manage their weapons and to use horses in battle, for they have frequented the court and been sent to England as hostages.'[69] If native Wales itself was not insulated from exterior cultural influences during the twelfth and thirteenth centuries, such influences must often have been even more strongly present in the March, which saw by far the greatest and most sustained immigration of foreign knights. Moreover, one would imagine that such Marcher lords as had landed interests and family connections in England and even further abroad would have shared in the ideal of chivalry, or at least been aware of it.

After *c.*1200, the Welsh chronicles record fewer massacres of castle garrisons. It may be merely a stylistic change: Welsh princes and Marcher lords are simply said to have 'gained possession of' castles, only sometimes explicitly after sieges.[70] In 1215, the year in which Rhys Ieuanc had the garrison of Hugh's Castle killed, those of Cardigan and Cilgerran castles surrendered to Llywelyn ab Iorwerth, apparently without forfeiting their lives.[71] In 1231, a Welsh force burned Cardigan 'up to the castle gate', slaying all the burgesses; but when in a later attack that year they breached the castle the garrison appear to have escaped with their lives.[72] In 1282, Gruffudd ap Maredudd and Rhys Fychan ap Rhys destroyed utterly the town and royal castle of Aberystwyth, but spared the garrison their lives 'because the days of the Passion were at hand'.[73]

It is even possible to point to some specific instances of Welsh and English captains conforming to the specific custom of granting garrisons conditional respite.[74] In 1196, the castle of Welshpool on the Severn was taken by the English with only one casualty, the rest of the garrison escaping 'free with their armour and weapons'. Later that year, Gwenwynwyn besieged it and obtained its surrender 'on the condition, too, that the garrison be given liberty to depart in safety and their raiment and arms with them'.[75] In 1210, Rhys Gryg 'gained possession of' the castle of Llandovery. Its Welsh garrison, 'having despaired of all help, surrendered the castle with sixteen steeds in it, on the feast of Mary in September, on condition that the garrison should have their bodies and all that was theirs safe'.[76] Two years later, Rhys Ieuanc granted conditional respite no less than twice, to the garrisons of Dinefwr and of Llandovery. On both occasions, he was at the head of armies containing both Welsh and English contingents.[77] In light of this, it seems quite probable that Rhys Ieuanc was also familiar with the right of storm, the principle that a garrison which had refused to surrender could be overrun without infringing the bounds of chivalry. The wording of one Welsh chronicle entry recording his destruction of the garrison of Hugh's Castle in 1215 may be highly relevant here. It specifically mentions that 'the garrison planned to defend the castle against him'.[78] Llywelyn ap Gruffudd, too, may well have been familiar with the customs governing castle warfare in England and France. In 1260, he seems to have spared the garrison after capturing Builth castle in a surprise night attack.[79] Two years later, he granted Roger Mortimer permission to go free after successfully besieging him in Cymaron castle.[80] Llywelyn would also appear to have allowed the garrison of Welshpool to live after they surrendered to him in 1274.[81]

The Welsh chronicles very often note that part of a defeated army or garrison was slain and part of it captured; indeed, it looks suspiciously like a standard phrase.[82] But at least in some cases, this phrase may reflect another instance of chivalrous behaviour in the March. In 1257, the barons and 'ordained knights' of a mixed Anglo-Welsh army were captured in a battle with the Welsh, while a great number of the 'host' were slain.[83] This certainly tallies well with the convention that the lives of noble opponents on the battlefield should be spared, even in cases where non-noble combatants were massacred.[84] So do the actions of Dafydd ap Gruffudd in 1281, when, after capturing Hawarden castle, he spared and imprisoned Roger Clifford, lord of the castle, along with one Payn Gamage, but slew all the rest of the garrison.[85]

Of course, the context of wider Anglo-Welsh relations meant that moderation might often have seemed advisable to both the Marchers and the Welsh; bloody attacks were always bound to constitute a greater provocation to the kings of England than petty raids or sieges that could be brought to a conclusion with the garrison alive. Nevertheless, it seems quite possible that the exercise of restraint was increasingly due to a growing acceptance of the norms which often governed warfare in England and France. After all, there are also unmistakable signs that chivalric culture made headway in the March. By the thirteenth century, the Marcher lords were great enthusiasts for heraldry,[86] and this enthusiasm eventually proved infectious. Morgan ap Lleision, lord of Afan, had not only assumed an Anglicized name. He was also dubbed a knight, married an English heiress and assumed a coat of arms which alluded to that of the Clare family, the lords of Glamorgan.[87] It is notable that the sons of Llywelyn ab Iorwerth both had a quartered shield of yellow and red, with four counter-changed lions; very probably this reflected the choice of arms their father had made.[88]

By the thirteenth century, at the latest, the Welsh princes were being included within the chivalric mindset of the Marchers as a matter of course. The world of the richest of Marcher ancestral romances, *Fouke le Fitz Waryn*, is partly a fantastical one, inhabited by giants and including imaginary journeys to faraway lands. Yet the text is far from being entirely divorced from thirteenth-century reality. It is remarkably familiar with the topography of the Welsh marches, particularly of Herefordshire and Shropshire. Also, though it is a tall tale, much of its cast is historical, even if individuals from different periods intermingle with each other and with purely fictional characters. Its intended audience doubtless included the Fitzwarin family of Whittington, and it clearly reflects that family's way of life as well as its appetite for an entertaining story. With all this borne in mind, *Fouke le Fitz Waryn* provides very direct evidence for the Marchers' view of the Welsh. It is revealed most directly by epithets, of course: Owain Cyfeiliog of Powys is described as 'a hardy and proud knight' (*un chevaler hardy e fer*), though his one deed in the story is to charge at the hero with couched lance and inflict a fairly serious injury on him.[89] The March certainly witnessed a clash of cultures in the twelfth and thirteenth centuries. But it remains to be seen how far it also was a place where cultures melded together.

The March was a culturally distinctive region, it would appear, primarily because it was a melting-pot. With perhaps a few deeply interesting exceptions, such as the 'd'Avenes' or perhaps the thirteenth-century 'de la Pole' lords of Powys,[90] the Welsh in the March remained in no doubt about their cultural affinity with the inhabitants of native Wales. As for the Normans and the English in the March, there are some indications that the position of these foreign settlers was not as straightforward. The case of Gerald of Wales suggests that he, for one, considered himself more or less a cultural outsider. He was fiercely proud, and defensive, of his family. But his family offered him no alternative to the Welsh and English identities.[91] There was no Marcher ethnicity. Perhaps there was no time for one to develop. More plausibly, the strength of the pre-existing identities, those of the English and the Welsh, would have prevented it in any case. True, the March was a region where identities were less certain, and institutions more malleable. Few other parts of Britain had a climate quite so conducive to the growth of cultural hybrids. Nevertheless, one cannot escape the impression that phenomena such as the Welsh knights' fees, mixed personal names, dual place-names or Welshmen performing castle-guard or acting as wardens of borough gates remained, on the whole, the exception rather than the rule. The March says much about the strength and homogeneity of the cultures which mingled in it. But that is a topic for another book.

Notes

1. *Bede's Ecclesiastical History of the English People*, ed. B. Colgrave and R. A. B. Mynors (Oxford, 1969). Bede chose the title himself.
2. P. Wormald, 'Bede, the *bretwaldas* and the origins of the *gens Anglorum*', in idem, D. Bullough and R. Collins (eds), *Ideal and Reality in Frankish and Anglo-Saxon Society: Studies Presented to John Michael Wallace-Hadrill* (Oxford, 1983), pp. 99–129; S. Foot, 'The making of *Angelcynn*: English identity before the Norman Conquest', *TRHS*, 6th ser., 6 (1996), 25–49; P. Wormald, '*Engla lond*: the making of an allegiance', *Journal of Historical Sociology*, 7/1 (1994), 1–24; T. Charles-Edwards, 'The making of nations in Britain and Ireland in the early Middle Ages', in R. Evans (ed.), *Lordship and Learning: Studies in Memory of Trevor Aston* (Woodbridge, 2004), pp. 11–37.
3. H. Pryce, 'British or Welsh? National identity in twelfth-century Wales', *English Historical Review*, 116/468 (2001), 775–801; Gerald of Wales, *Journey/Description*, pp. 231–2 (*Description*, i, 8).
4. D. Broun, 'Defining Scotland and the Scots before the Wars of Independence', in D. Broun, R. J. Finlay and M. Lynch (eds), *Image and Identity: The Making and Remaking of Scotland through the Ages* (Edinburgh, 1997), pp. 4–17.
5. Gillingham, *The English in the Twelfth Century*; H. M. Thomas, *The English and the Normans: Ethnic Hostility, Assimilation, and Identity, 1066–c.1220* (Oxford, 2003).
6. For 'Frenchmen', cf. *Brut*, eg. pp. 198–9, annal for 1213. For references to Normans, cf. *Brut*, pp. 114–15 (annal for 1136), pp. 116–17 (annal for 1137, referring to the late eleventh century) and pp. 140–1 (annal for 1159).
7. *Brut*, e.g. pp. 92–3 (annal for 1116); an army invading Wales in 1159 was said to contain 'Frenchmen and Normans and Flemings and Saxons and Welshmen' (*Brut*, pp. 140–1).
8. Mason, 'Roger de Montgomery and his sons', 1–28; cf. also idem in *ODNB*; cf. Bartlett, *Making of Europe*, ch. 2, esp. pp. 25–8 on the international exploits of the lords of Joinville in France.
9. *Regesta regum Anglo-Normannorum: Acta of William I*, ed. Bates, no. 281.
10. Thomas, *The English and Normans*, ch. 3.
11. It is striking that the medieval Latin life of Gruffudd ap Cynan refers to Henry I's older brother and predecessor, William Rufus, who was king of England from 1087 to 1100, as an 'Englishman' ('Anglus') leading an army of 'Frenchmen': *Vita Griffini Filii Conani*, ed. Russell, §25, sentences 6, 7 and 9 (pp. 78–9).
12. Richard fitz Nigel, *Dialogus de scaccario*, ed. C. Johnson et al., rev. edn (Oxford, 1983), pp. 53–4; Gillingham, *The English in the Twelfth Century*, pp. 123–32, 140.
13. Gerald of Wales, *The History and Topography of Ireland*, trans. L. Thorpe (1951, rev. edn, 1982), p. 119.
14. Gerald of Wales, *Journey/Description*, p. 149 (*Journey*, i, 12).
15. First preface to *Symbolum electorum*, *Giraldi Cambrensis opera*, ed. J. S. Brewer, J. F. Dimock and G. F. Warner (8 vols, RS, 1861–91), viii, p. lviii.

[16] *Giraldus, De invectionibus*, ed. Davies, p. 93 (i, 4).
[17] Gerald of Wales, *Journey/Description*, p. 149 (*Journey*, i, 12); cf. *Brut*, pp. 82–3. Nest was the daughter of Rhys ap Tewdwr, king of Deheubarth (d. 1093).
[18] *Brut*, pp. 164–5.
[19] *Expugnatio Hibernica: The Conquest of Ireland by Giraldus Cambrensis*, ed. and trans. A. B. Scott and F. X. Martin (Dublin, 1978), bk i, ch. 23. On the identity of the English in Ireland cf. J. F. Lydon, 'The middle nation', in idem (ed.), *The English in Medieval Ireland* (Dublin, 1984), pp. 1–26; R. Frame, '"Les Engleys nées en Irlande": the English political identity in medieval Ireland', *TRHS*, 6th ser., 3 (1993), 83–103.
[20] *Episcopal Acts and Cognate Documents Relating to Welsh Dioceses, 1066–1272*, ed. J. C. Davies (2 vols, Cardiff, 1946–8), i, 259 (D. 121).
[21] *Irish Historical Documents*, ed. Curtis and McDowell, pp. 37–8.
[22] S. Duffy, 'The problem of degeneracy', in J. F. Lydon (ed.), *Law and Disorder in Thirteenth-Century Ireland: The Dublin Parliament of 1297* (Dublin, 1997), pp. 87–106.
[23] For universal saints, cf. Bartlett, *Making of Europe*, pp. 270–4; on St David's cf. *The Song of Dermot and the Earl: An Old French Poem*, ed. and trans. G. H. Orpen (Oxford, 1892; repr. Felinfach, 1994), ll. 3440–53; new edn: *The Deeds of the Normans in Ireland: La Geste des Engleis en Yrlande*, ed. E. Mulally (Dublin, 2002).
[24] Though cf. D. Carpenter, *Struggle for Mastery*, pp. 19–22; M. Lieberman, 'The English and the Welsh in *Fouke le Fitz Waryn*', *Thirteenth-Century England*, 12 (Woodbridge, forthcoming).
[25] Cf. D. Postles and J. T. Rosenthal (eds), *Studies on the Personal Name in Later Medieval England and Wales* (Kalamazoo, MI, 2006), which contains contributions on the high medieval period.
[26] Gerald of Wales, *Journey/Description*, pp. 88–9 (*Journey*, i, 2).
[27] Gerald of Wales, *Expugnatio Hibernica*, ed. Scott and Martin, pp. 36–9 and n. 43.
[28] For example, *Cartae*, i, no. 169; cf. Lieberman, 'Anglicization in high medieval Wales', 19–20, 26.
[29] M. Griffiths, 'Native society on the Anglo-Norman frontier: the evidence of the Margam charters', *WHR*, 14 (1989), esp. 183–6, the map on 189 and the genealogical diagram on 215.
[30] *Cartae*, ii, 238. On the Welsh tenurial unit called *gwely* or *gafael*, cf. Davies, *Age of Conquest*, pp. 125–7; T. Charles-Edwards, *Early Irish and Welsh Kinship* (Oxford, 1993), pp. 226–56.
[31] Griffiths, 'Native society', 184–5.
[32] Davies, *Lordship and Society*, pp. 417–18; *Cartae*, iv, no. 983, p. 1245.
[33] Gerald of Wales, *Journey/Description*, pp. 75, 114, 186 (*Journey*, i, 1, in Radnor; i, 5, in Usk; ii, 7, on Anglesey).
[34] *Giraldi opera*, viii, 180–1 (*De principis instructione*, ii, 12).
[35] *Calendar of Inquisitions Miscellaneous*, pp. 508–10.
[36] *The Register of Thomas de Cantilupe, Bishop of Hereford (AD. 1275–1282)*, ed. R. G. Griffiths and W. W. Capes (Hereford, 1906), pp. 103–4.

[37] Giraldus Cambrensis, *Speculum duorum: or, a Mirror of Two Men*, ed. Y. Lefèvre and R. B. C. Huygen, trans. B. Dawson, gen. ed. M. Richter (Cardiff, 1974), pp. 36–7.
[38] B. G. Charles, 'The Welsh, their language and placenames in Archenfield and Oswestry', in *Angles and Britons: O'Donnell Lectures* (Cardiff, 1963), p. 93.
[39] Holt, *Magna Carta*, app. 6, esp. pp. 467–9 (clause 56 of the 1215 text).
[40] Cf. R. R. Davies, 'The law of the March', *WHR*, 5/1 (1970), 1–30, on whose findings this paragraph is based; see also idem, 'Laws and customs', 1–23.
[41] Bartlett, *Making of Europe*, ch. 8.
[42] R. R. Davies, 'Law and national identity in thirteenth-century Wales', in R. R. Davies, R. A. Griffiths, I. G. Jones and K. O. Morgan (eds), *Welsh Society and Nationhood: Historical Essays Presented to Glanmor Williams* (Cardiff, 1984), pp. 51–69.
[43] Davies, 'Laws and customs'.
[44] Davies, *Lordship and Society*, p. 76.
[45] W. Rees, *A Map of South Wales and the Border in the Fourteenth Century* (Ordnance Survey, 1932).
[46] *Calendar of Inquisitions Post Mortem*, vol. 5, *Edward II* (London, 1908), no. 538, p. 335.
[47] Ibid., p. 337.
[48] *Brut*, pp. 48–9.
[49] Strickland, *War and Chivalry*; J. Gillingham, '1066 and the introduction of chivalry into England', in G. Garnett and J. Hudson (eds), *Law and Government in Medieval England and Normandy: Essays in Honour of Sir James Holt* (Cambridge, 1994), pp. 31–55; see also idem, 'Conquering the barbarians: war and chivalry in twelfth-century Britain', *Haskins Society Journal*, 4 (1993 for 1992), 67–84; repr. in idem, *The English in the Twelfth Century*, pp. 41–58 and 209–31; idem, 'Killing and mutilating political enemies in the British Isles from the late twelfth to the early fourteenth century: a comparative study', in Smith (ed.), *Britain and Ireland, 900–1300*, pp. 114–34; idem, '"Holding to the rules of war (*bellica iura tenentes*)": right conduct before, during, and after battle in north-western Europe in the eleventh century', *Anglo-Norman Studies*, 29 (2007) (R. Allen Brown Memorial Lecture), 2–15.
[50] *EHD*, ii, 244.
[51] Strickland, *War and Chivalry*, p. 1; on the 'right of storm', ibid., pp. 222–4.
[52] *The Chronicle of John, Prior of Hexham*, in *The Priory of Hexham, its Chroniclers, Endowments and Annals*, ed. J. Raine (2 vols, Durham, 1868); i, 118; *The Acts of King Stephen, etc., by Richard of Hexham*, in *The Priory of Hexham*, ed. Raine, i, 100; cf. Strickland, *War and Chivalry*, p. 219.
[53] *The Chronicle of John, Prior of Hexham*, ed. Raine, i, 82–3; *The Acts of King Stephen, etc., by Richard of Hexham*, ed. Raine, i, 116; cf. Strickland, *War and Chivalry*, pp. 314–15.
[54] Gerald of Wales, *Journey/Description*, pp. 268–9 (*Description*, ii, 8). The passage appears almost verbatim in bk 2, ch. 38 of *Expugnatio Hibernica*. Cf. Gerald of Wales, *Expugnatio Hibernica*, ed. Scott and Martin, pp. 244–9.

[55] For reasons not to take Gerald's views on the brutality of Marcher warfare at face value cf. S. Davies, *Welsh Military Institutions, 633–1283* (Cardiff, 2004).
[56] R. R. Davies, 'The survival of the bloodfeud in medieval Wales', *History: The Journal of the Historical Association*, 54 (1969), 338–57.
[57] Gerald of Wales, *Journey/Description*, pp. 96 (*Journey*, i, 2), 201 (*Journey*, ii, 12); cf. his general comment on the vindictiveness of the Welsh – and of their saints – on p. 189 (*Journey*, ii, 7).
[58] Cf. the genealogical diagram in Davies, *Age of Conquest*, p. 60.
[59] *Brut*, pp. 74–5.
[60] Strickland, *War and Chivalry*, esp. ch. 6.
[61] *Orderic*, ed. Chibnall, iv, 138–9.
[62] *Brut*, pp. 34–5.
[63] Ibid., pp. 86–95.
[64] Ibid., pp. 148–9.
[65] Gerald of Wales, *Journey/Description*, p. 108 (*Journey*, i, 4).
[66] *Brut*, pp. 176–7.
[67] On this document cf. 'An early charter of the abbey of Cwmhir', ed. Charles; and comments in Smith, 'The middle March', 80–1.
[68] *Brut*, pp. 214–17.
[69] Gerald of Wales, *Journey/Description*, p. 267 (*Description*, ii, 7).
[70] For examples, cf. *Brut*, pp. 182–5; 194–5 (s. a. 1212: Llywelyn's army is driven off by John 'when they were gaining possession of the castle of Mathrafal').
[71] *Brut*, pp. 204–5.
[72] Ibid., pp. 230–1.
[73] Ibid., pp. 268–71.
[74] On grants of conditional respite cf. Strickland, *War and Chivalry*, pp. 208–12.
[75] *Brut*, pp. 176–7.
[76] Ibid., pp. 188–9.
[77] Ibid., pp. 196–9. Note that the Welsh chronicle records Welsh and 'French' contingents.
[78] *Brut*, pp. 203–4.
[79] Ibid., pp. 250–1.
[80] Ibid., pp. 252–3.
[81] Ibid., pp. 260–1.
[82] For examples, cf. ibid., pp. 196–7 (s.a. 1212); battle of Lincoln in 1215; pp. 218–19 (the siege of Damietta in 1217); or ibid., pp. 246–7 (the battle of Bryn Derwin between Llywelyn ap Gruffudd and his brothers Owain and Dafydd in 1255).
[83] Ibid., pp. 248–9.
[84] Strickland, *War and Chivalry*, esp. pp. 176–82 and ch. 10.
[85] *Brut*, pp. 268–9.
[86] For examples cf. *Rolls of Arms, Henry III*, ed. T. D. Tremlett (London, 1967), pp. 18 (William the Marshal, d. 1219); 55, 64 (Gilbert de Clare, d. 1230); 121 (Roger Mortimer of Wigmore, d. 1282); 132 (John Fitzalan, d. 1267, who assumed the arms of Hugh d'Aubigny, the earl of Arundel).
[87] *GCH*, iii, 51–2; *Cartae*, ii, no. 533, p. 543 (1247) and no. 537, pp. 561–2 (1249) show Leison, son of Morgan, attending the county court; cf. *Cartae*, iii, no. 809,

p. 924 for Clark's suggestion that his nephew, also Leison ap Morgan, had adopted 'd'Avene'. Note that this charter is in Latin. For Welsh heraldry in general cf. M. P. Siddons, *The Development of Welsh Heraldry* (4 vols, Aberystwyth, 1991–2006).

[88] *Rolls of Arms: Henry III*, pp. 69–70, 71.; cf. D. Crouch, *The Image of Aristocracy in Britain, 1000–1300* (London, 1992), p. 241. There appears to be no contemporary evidence for the heraldic arms of Llywelyn ab Iorwerth: Siddons, *Welsh Heraldry*, i, 1 and 280.

[89] *Fouke*, ed. Hathaway et al., p. 20, ll. 20–3.

[90] On whom cf. Davies, *Lordship and Society*, e.g. p. 31.

[91] For an illuminating debate on this point cf. Bartlett, *Gerald of Wales*, ch. 1, esp. pp. 20–5; and J. Gillingham, 'The English invasion of Ireland', in B. Bradshaw, A. Hadfield and W. Maley (eds), *Representing Ireland: Literature and the Origins of Conflict* (Cambridge, 1993), pp. 24–42; repr. in Gillingham, *The English in the Twelfth Century*, pp. 145–60, esp. 155–7.

5

Kingdoms, Countries and Marches: the Context of the British Isles

The histories of Wales, of England and of Scotland all begin during the medieval period. But Wales, England and Scotland clearly began in different ways. It is enough to consider the basic theme of territorial power. An important part of the creation of England and of Scotland was the establishment of one king for England and one for Scotland, and the consolidation of their grip on significant parts of Britain. Wales, being far more politically fragmented than either England or Scotland, did not have a comparably straightforward history as a single kingdom. All medieval political entities of Britain were not alike. Moreover, of course, there were several others besides Wales, England and Scotland. The kingdom of the Picts had been one.[1] The kingdom of Cumbria had a history stretching back to the sixth century; like Wales, it took shape in a part of Britain which remained Brittonic even after the arrival of the Germanic Angles, Saxons and Jutes. The kingdom of Cumbria, however, only survived until the eleventh century. Its last king died, it is thought, in 1018, in the battle of Carham-on-Tweed; Cumbria was certainly annexed by the king of Scots soon after, and was never revived as a separate polity. In 1092 it was partitioned between Scotland and England.[2] The case of Cumbria is a cautionary tale. There was nothing inevitable about the making of any of the kingdoms and countries of medieval Europe, and those of medieval Britain were no exception to this rule.[3]

The creation of Britain's kingdoms and countries was of course linked to the shaping of the Welsh, Scots and English identities. The two topics are equally intricate. But the March of Wales is as illuminating for the history of Britain's countries as it is for its 'ethnic' identities. As has been seen, the identities of the Welsh, the Normans and the English in Britain are strikingly highlighted in the March. But the March is also a showcase for the shaping of Wales and, even more particularly, of England. For instance, in the thirteenth century and up until 1536 the singular 'constitutional' position of the March tells us something about the medieval English 'state'. That 'state' is rightly regarded as the precocious forerunner among the medieval governmental systems of Europe. Yet the persistence of Marcher lordships on its frontier with the Principality of Wales meant that even medieval England did not have entirely clearly delineated boundaries.[4] As for Wales, the existence of the March, so Rees Davies has argued, bore decisively on the way in which the concept of 'Wales' itself was reforged and deployed in the thirteenth century, particularly by the princes of Gwynedd.[5]

Some general reflections may illustrate this argument further. The margins of politically, culturally or administratively defined territories often have as much to reveal as the centres of those territories. In other words, a good way of discussing the nature of a country, a kingdom, a state or an empire is to look at its frontiers. The building of the Great Walls of China means that the power of the Chinese empire during two thousand years of its history cannot be fully appreciated without taking into account its northern frontier.[6] Hadrian's Wall, the Antonine Wall and the other Roman frontiers in north Britain, along with the rest of the Roman *limes* fortifications, along the Rhine and the Danube, in the Near East and in Africa, reflect not only the final extent but the nature of the Roman empire.[7] To take an example from more recent times, the early history of the United States of America has famously, if controversially, been written entirely as the history of an advancing 'Frontier'.[8] Different kinds of frontiers tell us different kinds of things. But there can be no doubt that the study of peripheries complements that of cores. Locating frontiers on the ground inevitably involves deciding what is being demarcated.

Such reflections suggest that the contrast between the March of Wales on the one hand and earlier manifestations of the Anglo-Welsh border on the other should reflect contrasts between Anglo-Saxon England and England after 1066, and between early and high medieval Wales. Certainly the importance of the Anglo-Welsh border to the shaping of England and of Wales has not been lost on historians. Their accounts of the making of those two countries have naturally been influenced by the fact that a monumental earth wall was built in the late eighth century roughly along what became the Anglo-Welsh frontier. Historians of Wales have also shown the importance of other factors, of the creation of a native culture, of the language and of the laws of Wales. But Offa's Dyke is generally agreed to have played an important role in creating the identity of the Welsh and the unity and distinctiveness of their country. The medieval Welsh laws themselves reflect that to some Welshmen, at least, the chief land-boundary of Wales was *Clawdd Offa*.[9]

The existence of Offa's Dyke means that archaeology plays a key role in recovering the early history, or perhaps rather the prehistory, of Wales and of England. Archaeologists, meanwhile, have recently challenged our understanding of Offa's Dyke as a frontier between the Welsh and the Anglo-Saxon kingdoms. After thirty years of fieldwork and excavation, David Hill and Margaret Worthington have recently proposed a radical solution to an old puzzle of Offa's Dyke.[10] Famously, Asser, the biographer of Alfred the Great, stated in the late ninth century that Offa had his dyke built along the Welsh frontier 'from sea to sea'; yet modern archaeologists have struggled to trace its course from coast to coast. It was believed for much of the twentieth century, following the work of Sir Cyril Fox, that the dyke survived in a virtually unbroken line along its central section, but that almost no trace of it could be found roughly to the north of what is now Shropshire or to the south of what is now Herefordshire. Along both sections, the long and difficult search for the remainder of the Dyke seemed to indicate that it had either been worn away over the centuries, or destroyed, or perhaps that there had always been gaps. Fox had put forward the idea that the area south of Hereford had been so densely wooded in the eighth century that it was rendered impassable. Hill and Worthington have dared to propose the radical solution to the mystery of the missing Dyke: that the Dyke built by Offa of Mercia did not reach 'from sea to sea' at all. In their view, Offa only built the well-preserved central section north and south of the Severn gap. The other earthworks, they concluded, were the result of separate efforts. Asser's statement about the length of Offa's Dyke was mere rhetorical flourish. Offa built his wall not as a barrier against all the Welsh, but against one Welsh kingdom, Powys.[11]

As has been seen, the Dyke predates by centuries the time when the inhabitants of what is now Wales began normally referring to themselves as 'Welsh' rather than 'British'.[12] It also now appears that the country that came to be called 'Wales' was never demarcated against the English by a single earth wall.[13] The Dyke is also central to one of the most remarkable arguments proposed by a scholar of Anglo-Saxon England in recent times: Professor James Campbell's case for seeing late Anglo-Saxon England as a nation-state. That case rests on the existence, by 1066, of 'an effective central authority, uniformly organised institutions, a national language, a national church, defined frontiers (admittedly with considerably fluidity in the north), and, above all, a strong sense of national identity'.[14] The most impressive documentary monument to 'the late Anglo-Saxon nation-state' is Domesday Book. Offa's Dyke, predating that document by almost three centuries, is evidence for the prehistory of the 'late Anglo-Saxon nation-state'; but it is important evidence, particularly for the prehistory of the institutions of that 'nation-state' and, of course, for one of its two frontiers.

As far as institutions are concerned, Offa's Dyke is evidence for the phenomenal capacity for organized effort of at least one early Anglo-Saxon kingdom. The king of Mercia was clearly able to muster thousands upon thousands of labourers, and to keep them at work at a huge but economically unproductive task for years, if not decades. This was almost certainly done, unimaginable as this may seem to us today, without the use of written instruments. The feat of building Offa's Dyke must have involved marshalling the populace, assessing its numbers and communicating with it. This alone is some reason to trace back to Offa's days the ancestry of the eleventh-century administrative machine of the English kingdom. A very direct and sustained control over a widely dispersed populace would already appear to have been feasible for Offa, who was king of Mercia from 757 to 796. What is more, such governance may well have been partly based on some of the same administrative tools which still remained in use in England in the eleventh century and indeed long afterwards. In particular, the division of land into units, notably for the purpose of taxation, may have survived into the eleventh century from very early on indeed. We know from early Anglo-Saxon documentary sources, from charters, laws and place-names, but also from the much-discussed 'Tribal Hidage', 'Burghal Hidage' and 'County Hidage', that such administrative territorial units existed long before Domesday Book, and that they were known as hides. Hidation of land may originally have followed the principle that a hide was the land that could be ploughed by a peasant family every year; later on, a hide was often equal to 120 acres. The carucate, or ploughland (from Latin *carruca*, 'plough'), of the Danelaw corresponds to the hides of southern England. The English hides had their parallels on the early medieval Continent, which is another indication of their antiquity. Offa's Dyke may be evidence that, in the eighth-century Anglo-Saxon kingdoms, hides already formed part of the basis for a sophisticated system of governance.[15] The Dyke, therefore, is also an essential piece in the puzzle of how the English 'state' could reach such an extraordinary level of development by 1066.

Three centuries separate Offa's Dyke from Domesday Book. As has been mentioned, the political boundary between the Anglo-Saxon and the Welsh kingdoms remained more or less in place from *c.*800 until 1066. Whatever the reasons, the late Anglo-Saxon 'state' never undertook the conquest of Wales in earnest. It retained two frontiers, one with the kingdom of the Scots and one with the Welsh kingdoms. This would lead one to expect that the way in which the Anglo-Welsh frontier changed between the building of Offa's Dyke and 1066 must bear witness to the rise of this 'Anglo-Saxon nation-state'. Of the evidence available for discussing this issue, that of Domesday Book is by far the most bountiful. Domesday reveals a wealth of detail about the situation in the later eleventh century; and in conjunction with earlier documents, it can also be used to illuminate the earlier history of the frontier.

This can perhaps be best illustrated by looking at institutions. The creation of the border shires, of Gloucestershire, Herefordshire, Shropshire and Cheshire, naturally transformed the frontier, at least from the Anglo-Saxon point of view. The origins of the English shires have been much debated; but it would appear most probable that the Mercian shires were created as part of a coordinated scheme, and on the model of the shires of Wessex.[16] A key date in the history of the border shires must therefore have been 918, when Edward the Elder, king of Wessex, began to rule Mercia directly. It would have been a natural step for the kings of Wessex to divide their newly acquired lands into manageable units (the shires) and place them under the authority of representatives (the shire-reeves or sheriffs). Whenever this was done, it was accomplished with remarkable thoroughness. By 1066, almost every Anglo-Saxon village in the borders was, for fiscal and judicial purposes, grouped with other villages into a hundred, and every hundred was part of a shire. In this system the borders of the hundreds and shires, rather than earth walls and rivers, had come to be synonymous with the Welsh frontier. From the English point of view, at least.

There is no better example to show the implications of this than the country to the south of Hereford, beyond the river Wye. In the early tenth century, Athelstan, king of the English, had fixed the Wye as the boundary of his kingdom with the Welsh.[17] Orderic Vitalis, who was born in Shropshire in 1075, considered that the Wye still 'separated the Welsh from the English' in 1138.[18] By 1066, there had, however, been significant migration and settlement of Englishmen across the Wye, beyond the frontier drawn by Athelstan. Moreover, this had not been merely a matter of the movement of people; they had brought with them, or been followed, by English institutions. Their estates were assessed in hides, and assigned to hundreds. What is more, there are indications that this had happened quite recently. The estates just beyond the Wye, in 'Dinedor' hundred, are assessed on the basis of regular units of three hides. This probably was because there had not yet been much time for them to be split up.[19]

Beyond this area of English settlement lay the Welsh district of Archenfield (Welsh Erging). This had been a part of the Welsh kingdom of Gwent in Athelstan's day. Even in 1066, it remained in the Welsh diocese of Llandaf in Morgannwg.[20] A late eleventh-century Welsh poem includes Archenfield within an imaginary tour of Wales.[21] Archenfield was still largely Welsh-populated in 1066, but it would appear to have come under English control at some point. It is listed in Domesday Book under its own heading.[22] It was not a hundred or part of any hundred, nor had it yet been hidated; that is, its Welsh settlements were assessed, too, but in 'ploughs', not hides. The Welsh of Archenfield were also treated differently in that they owed customary renders of honey and of sheep. The bloodfeud conventions of native Welsh society prevailed: 'if a Welshman kills a Welshman, the relatives of the slain meet together, and plunder the slayer and his kin, and burn their houses until on the morrow at about noon the corpse of the dead man is buried'.[23] As ancient as such customs may have been, in English-controlled Archenfield they had, by 1066, been modified: the king of England laid claim to a third of the plunder taken by the 'relatives of the slain'. The district south of the Wye, then, displays different stages in a process that went far beyond the mere settlement of Englishmen. The parts which lay just beyond the Wye had effectively already become integrated into Herefordshire. By contrast, Archenfield had come under English control; but it had not yet been settled by Englishmen, nor had English institutions made much headway there.

On the northern Welsh coast, in what was then the western part of Cheshire, the situation was comparable. Here, Offa's Dyke, and presumably also Wat's Dyke, had at one time marked the boundary of English settlement. In 1086, Wat's Dyke still divided hidated land to the east from unhidated land to the west. But the western boundary of Cheshire had, by 1066, been extended considerably beyond Wat's Dyke. At the time, Cheshire included Englefield: although that territory was unhidated, it had been annexed to the hundred of Ati's Cross. In 1086, Englefield consisted of the Alun valley (Bistre) and of the great estate centred on Rhuddlan.[24] This had been disputed territory for centuries. In 1066, it had probably been brought under English control quite recently. As was the case in 'Dinedor' hundred south of the Wye, this had brought with it the advance of the building blocks of the English 'state', to wit, the hundred and the shire. The only difference was that the hide had yet to follow; as yet, in Englefield, even Norman- and English-held land was assessed in 'ploughs'.

It does appear, then, that the Welsh frontier might tell us much about the rise of the 'late Anglo-Saxon nation-state'. The close link between the advance of English settlers and of the typical administrative tools of the English 'state' powerfully illustrates how well-developed those tools were. The English 'state' was so uniformly organized that, at its Welsh border, its institutions naturally followed English settlers moving into Welsh territory. It is also notable, however, that the English 'state' was still flexible enough to ingest Welsh-settled territories.[25] Perhaps this was a sign that it was still at an early stage in its development, when experiments were easier. Eleventh-century England may have been a nation-state; but it appeared to be able and willing to expand into Wales, if by gradual encroachment rather than by military conquest. Thus, it does seem that Archenfield and Englefield have to be considered in a very wide context: the creation of the 'state' of the English, the 'late Anglo-Saxon nation-state'.

It is abundantly clear that early Norman encroachment on Welsh territory after 1066 did not expand the English 'state' into Wales. The border earls, William fitz Osbern, Roger de Montgomery, Hugh the Fat and their followers were not in the business of turning bits of Wales into England. They were interested in grabbing land for themselves, and their kings appear not to have objected. In some places, it is true, the advance of the Normans actually appears to have brought with it the advance of English institutions. The most striking early example is the Norman conquest of part of the Welsh kingdom of Morgannwg. As has been seen, the violent death of Rhys ap Tewdwr in 1093 probably encouraged the Norman inroads into Brycheiniog, Ceredigion and Dyfed; and the same was very possibly true of those into Morgannwg. These latter were led by one Robert fitz Hamo, who came from the Calvados area of Normandy. In 1107, Robert died from a wound to the head which caused him debilitating brain damage, and which he had received two years earlier at the siege of Falaise. In the short time he had at his disposal between seizing land in Morgannwg and losing his senses, he had founded the *comitatus*, the county or shire of Glamorgan. Indeed, Glamorgan had its own sheriff by 1102.[26] Unlike the sheriffs of the

English shires, however, this new sheriff was an appointee of fitz Hamo's rather than the king of England's. He did not report to the royal exchequer but to his Norman lord at Cardiff. Thus, fitz Hamo's case reveals that quintessentially English institutions were indeed very rapidly transplanted into Wales after 1066. But it also shows that this was not equivalent to an expansion of the English 'state'. The sheriff of Glamorgan took up his duties as an agent of seignorial not royal control. Nor was the sheriff the only institution characteristic of the English 'nation-state' which was imported by the lords of Cardiff. Kenfig castle came to have a 'hundred' attached to it; by the second half of the twelfth century, Robert, then sheriff of Glamorgan, presided over an assembly which is described as the 'Welsh hundred of the county of Margam'.[27] On English manors, the judicial courts held by the lord for the tenants were often referred to as hallmoots or halmotes; by the fourteenth century, and probably much earlier, Clun lordship had a 'hallmoot of the Welsh' for its Welsh bondsmen.[28] But these were, clearly, colonial imports. From the outset, the Norman conquests in Wales were geared towards the creation of Marcher lordships rather than of new English shires. Those conquests constituted a rude disruption to the slow but steady process of expansion that can be discerned in the Domesday folios for Archenfield and Englefield.

Thus, the borders of the shires had, by 1086, largely held fast despite the extension of Norman power into Wales. But part of the reason for this may well have been that expansion was driven not by the king himself, but by his barons. The one surviving Pipe Roll for the reign of Henry I, that for 1129–30, suggests that perhaps the extent of the Norman kingdom of England was not set in stone at the period. Pembroke and Carmarthen rendered accounts to the royal exchequer because Henry I had seized those territories (Pembroke, as mentioned, was seized after its forfeiture by Arnulf of Montgomery in 1102; the royal castle at Carmarthen was built soon afterwards).[29] There was a royal sheriff at Pembroke in that year named Hait, who was probably a Fleming; and there were other royal officials, foresters and beadles, and most remarkably, a royal moneyer with the Irish name of Gillopatric. 'Pembroc' is not referred to as a county in this document, but that does not mean it was not regarded as one. The Pipe Roll also records the payment into the royal treasury of one pound owed for malicious prosecution by one of the Flemings of Pembroke. This almost certainly occurred in a court presided over by sheriff Hait: effectively a county court of Pembroke.[30] The entry for Carmarthen reveals perhaps a different stage of a similar development. Carmarthen was not a shire at this period (in any case, no sheriff is mentioned); it is referred to as an 'honor', that is, a royal lordship.[31] The evidence for Pembroke and Carmarthen in the late 1120s perhaps suggests that there was no objection in principle to Welsh territories being included routinely within the central administration of the kingdom of England. Indeed, one may wonder if the first Norman kings might have extended the English 'state' into Wales had they not left the conquest of Welsh territory to others. It is of course also possible that Carmarthen and Pembroke were thought of as royal lordships rather than parts of the English 'state'. Not inconceivably, however, a window of opportunity for the further expansion of that 'state' into Wales had been opened by the Norman conquest of England, and had not yet quite closed by the end of Henry I's reign.

If so, it was soon to close, and to remain firmly closed. By *c.* 1300, Rees Davies has recently argued, the Englishness of the English 'state' had reached new heights. In particular, according to this view, there were ever clearer signs that the English 'state' operated on the assumption that it existed only for Englishmen.[32] Thus, it retained the close association of English settlers and English institutions characteristic of the late Anglo-Saxon 'state', but lacked the latter's flexibility in incorporating territories not settled by Englishmen. The entrenchment of the idea that the English kingdom was exclusively the 'state' of the English people was a many-faceted process bearing on the history of four countries. It involved elements as disparate as the centralization of the English king's bureaucracy and the literary creation of a mythology concerning England's origins. It is a complex story. But one revealing strand in it can be unravelled by comparing the north of England in the later twelfth and early thirteenth centuries with the experience of Ireland. Both these territories experienced the power of the English king to an unprecedented extent at that period. But rather different treatments were meted out to them. After 1157, when Henry II intimidated the Scottish king Malcolm IV into yielding up the northern counties, no effort was spared to achieve their full integration within the English 'state'. That goal was still far from being attained at the end of John's reign. Henry I had had local justiciars in the northern counties,[33] but royal officials rarely ventured there on business, even during the first half of Henry II's reign. It was only after the rebellion of Henry II's sons in 1173–4, in which the king of Scots and several northern barons had been involved, that the English kings acted with more determination. In the last quarter of the twelfth century, Cumberland and Westmorland finally began to function as shires (Westmorland received a sheriff in 1177–8). The kings themselves and their justices in eyre began to pay far more regular visits. This, coupled of course with heavy fiscal demands on a region quite unaccustomed to such impositions, very directly explains the leading role played by the northern aristocracy in the rebellion against John.[34] But that rebellion itself was a rebellion of England's barons against their king. In 1215, in the year John was forced to sign Magna Carta, what was at issue was the rights of the English king in his kingdom. Therefore, the rebellion, and especially the leading role played in it by the northern barons, indeed confirmed that the northern counties were part of that kingdom.

At precisely the same period Ireland, too, was acquired, nominally, by the English kings. In 1171–2, Henry II intervened, as has been seen, in the rapid process of territorial conquest on which the southern Marchers had embarked. He proclaimed his son John king of Ireland in 1177, and sent him there on a sort of embassy in 1185 (during which, admittedly, the entourage of the 18-year-old John only managed to antagonize the Irish kings by pulling 'some of them about by their beards, which were large and flowing according to the native custom').[35] As in the northern counties of England, English institutions soon began to be exported to Ireland. Henry II already had officials there; Hugh de Lacy acted as the king's deputy from 1172 (until 1186, when Hugh was decapitated by an Irishman while campaigning in westernmost Meath). By the time John became king, the foundations for a dedicated administrative structure for Ireland had already been laid; an exchequer for Ireland was operating, filling the coffers of the English crown.[36] Our first record of 'the king's court in Ireland' dates to 1199, the year of John's accession.[37] As king of England and lord of Ireland, John was already able to call on the services of sheriffs based at Dublin, Waterford (including Cork) and Munster. In 1204, John ordered a strong castle at Dublin to be built to house the royal treasury. After he seized the de Lacy lordships of Meath and Ulster, he could also raise revenues through the stewards responsible for those provinces. The king's writ ran in the great English lordship of Leinster, and the magnates there were responsible for collecting his dues. The king's chief governor in Ireland, normally referred to as 'justiciar', headed up a judiciary system through which the common law of England was administered in Ireland. After 1210, a register of writs for the use of the king's officials was dispatched to Ireland (this was arguably a precursor to the Statute of Rhuddlan of 1284, which was to specify the laws to apply in the Principality of Wales).[38] The 1217 version of Magna Carta was transferred to Ireland, that is, the king of England and his council decreed that its provisions should be enforced there.[39] By 1218 at the latest there were justices itinerant in addition to the chief governor himself.

The royal lordship of Ireland developed apace throughout the thirteenth century. By 1300, it was governed in the king's absence by a justiciar advised by a council and supported by a chancery. The exchequer was presided over by a treasurer and run by barons of the exchequer, chamberlains and lesser officers. There were two central courts of justice, the justiciar's bench, which like the chancery was itinerant, and the common bench, which sat at Dublin. The justiciar had by this time long been in the habit of summoning parliaments (like the one which passed the laws against degeneracy in 1297); at local level shires had proliferated, with their county courts, sheriffs, coroners and other officers. The shires were interspersed with great liberties held by English barons. But the creation of the lordship of Ireland was achieved by duplicating the institutions of the English 'state'.

This greatly augmented the lands of the English crown. But it was no expansion of England or of the English 'state'. The lordship of Ireland was separately administered. What is more, that lordship may have been created by the duplication of English institutions; but those institutions tended to be reserved to the English in Ireland. It was not merely a matter of paranoid legislation against degeneracy. The law of England was applied in Ireland, but not, as a rule, in cases between Irishmen.[40] It was a rule which became ever stricter during the thirteenth and fourteenth centuries, even though in the late 1270s Irish ecclesiastics campaigned for English law to be generally extended to the Irish.[41] The example of law hints at a wider picture. In general, it would appear, the expansion of English royal power throughout the British Isles entailed the spread of institutions which were increasingly perceived to be reserved for the English. On the one hand, English power was being projected ever further throughout the British Isles. On the other, it did so on terms which favoured the domination rather than the integration of native societies. Needless to say, this hampered the inclusion of native societies within a single polity. The self-perception of the English 'state' helped to prevent the creation of a single, united kingdom of the British Isles during the medieval period. What Edward I presided over towards the end of his reign was an English empire in the British Isles.[42]

The creation of the March of Wales fits neatly into this account of how the English 'state' developed between 1066 and *c.*1300. By the latter date, of course, the Marcher lords were themselves actively opposing the expansion of the English 'state' westwards into Wales. They were even pushing it eastwards, insofar as they were successful at withdrawing English territory into the March. Yet perhaps it could be argued that the Marcher lordships developed in line with the English kingdom. They too inherited from the 'late Anglo-Saxon nation-state' the close link between foreign settlers and foreign institutions; and they too, on the whole, failed to integrate Welshmen and Englishmen within single administrative bodies. In the March, ethnic groups were treated as distinct entities, each with their own place in an administrative framework. That framework was imposed not by the king of England but by the Marcher lords. But it may well be that Englishries and Welshries were established because of a mindset which developed in lockstep in the March as well as England. Certainly the distinction in the March between the Welsh and the new settlers was upheld not by the Marcher lords alone. All colonists, peasants, monks and burgesses, Normans, Flemings and English alike, shared a sense of being different from the Welsh. In 1188, Gerald remembered, when the Third Crusade was being preached at Llandaf in Glamorgan, the 'English stood on one side and the Welsh on the other; and from each nation many took the Cross'.[43] The sometimes not so tacit assumptions which prevented the English 'state' from including its neighbours in the British Isles are mirrored in the administrative, legal and social divisions of the March.

Of course, if the English 'state' indeed became more ethnically exclusive during the thirteenth century, then that would suggest that it became less likely to expand into the March; or, in any case, into the Welsh-populated part of the March. Given that the Marchers fought tooth and nail to prevent that happening anyway, it is actually quite difficult to tell whether any ethnic exclusivity was displayed by the agents of the English 'state' in their dealings with the Marcher lordships. But one or two pointers might be mentioned. The English 'state' became embroiled in several minor but telling ambiguities on its border with Wales. The lordship of Montgomery, though it escheated permanently to the crown in 1207, and though it bordered directly on the hundreds of Shropshire, was never included within that county. Instead, after 1536–42 it became part of the shire to which it lent its name, the only shire in Britain to be named after a castle in Normandy. One wonders if this was, in part, because it lay mostly beyond Offa's Dyke in Welsh-populated territory.

Other examples are provided by the fiscal history of the March. The Welsh of Archenfield paid their share of Henry III's tax of a fifteenth on movables in 1225. Later, however, they were able to claim exemption from English taxes by asserting that Archenfield was part of the Welsh March.[44] It is tempting to think that such an assertion was more easily accepted at the later date because by then the ethnicity of Archenfield's population made it less likely for them to be taxed by the English 'state' anyway. Our evidence is fuller for the early 1290s. In 1290, the English Parliament granted Edward I permission to levy a tax on England, to finance a campaign in Gascony; a year later, that grant was extended to include, for the first time, Wales and the March.[45] Unsurprisingly, collecting those taxes did not prove straightforward. Edmund Mortimer was accused of evading them and had to prove before royal magistrates that he had indeed allowed the English tax to be levied on his lands in Shropshire and the Welsh tax on his Marcher lordship of Wigmore.[46] These episodes demonstrate the phenomenal power of the English 'state' in micro-managing even parts of Britain which were remote from its south-eastern heartland. At the same time, they may be evidence that it was equally effective and consistent about excluding Welsh-populated territories from its operation. It is, of course, impossible to be certain that the English 'state' would not have expanded further into Wales had it not been for the Marcher lords. But such examples suggest that perhaps it might not have. It may be that, by the thirteenth century, the Marcher lords were not alone responsible for preventing the expansion of the English 'state'.

The long-term history of the Welsh border provides a unique perspective on the history of the English 'state'; and the history of the English 'state' adds a further dimension to the making of the March. Without Offa's Dyke, the prehistories of Wales and of England would have to be written very differently; the latest archaeological investigations suggest that they may have to be rewritten. In the centuries leading up to 1066, no full-scale conquest of Wales was undertaken by the English (the emphasis was on the conquest of Danish-held Anglo-Saxon kingdoms). But it would seem that at some point before 1066, at the very time when the 'Anglo-Saxon nation-state' was taking shape, that 'state' was gradually expanding westwards into Welsh territory. It was doing so in what might be called an organic fashion. In places like Archenfield, and west of Chester, English settlement brought with it, as a matter of course, the building blocks of the English 'state', the hides and the hundred. There is no better illustration of how deeply ingrained these institutions had become in Anglo-Saxon society by the eleventh century. The movement of English settlers into Wales would, it seems, naturally have led to the creation of new shires or the expansion of existing ones. There were no isolated English colonies in Wales. What were occurring along this relatively stable border were the 'natural' fluctuations of settlement and migration that might be expected over the long term between two premodern polities. It was just that with English settlement and migration came English institutions. At the same time, districts like Archenfield may reveal that there was still room for compromise, and that the 'Anglo-Saxon nation-state' was still flexible enough to incorporate Welsh-inhabited territory.

This organic growth of the English 'state' was rudely cut short by the Norman conquest of England. It was never to resume. However, there is some reason to believe that this course of events was not inevitable. Until 1130, in any case, the English kingdom and its exchequer quite routinely dealt with Norman-conquered territories in Wales in much the same way as it did with Norman-conquered England, so long as those territories were in royal hands. The project of annexing Welsh territory was not close to the heart of any Norman king of England – at least not as close as it was to the hearts of the early Marchers. Otherwise the borders of the English kingdom, and of Wales, might have been drawn very differently.

It would be interesting to know, also, in what ways the history of the March may have been affected by the barriers which the medieval English 'state' built against the inclusion of those who were not English. Perhaps the definition of Marcher liberties was taking place at the very time that the English 'state' was defining itself in new ways. Certainly the very long term will need to be considered if we are to locate the place of the March in the history of how the countries of Britain were created. Like the kingdom of Cumbria, as a political entity the March disappeared without a trace. Perhaps this is in itself a most significant clue. It may be that in the history of the countries of Britain, the March was an anomaly. It was not so much that the March was politically fragmented; that was true of Wales proper too. But, as was argued in the last chapter, the March was a region of multiple identities; its inhabitants developed no identity of their own to rival the options of being either Welsh or English. Perhaps in the long term, this made it unlikely that the March would leave a lasting impression on the political map of Britain.

Notes

[1] K. Forsyth, 'Origins: Scotland to 1100', in J. Wormald (ed.), *Scotland: A History* (Oxford, 2005), pp. 1–37.
[2] A. A. M. Duncan, *Scotland: The Making of the Kingdom* (Edinburgh, 1975; repr. 1996), p. 93; idem, *The Kingship of the Scots, 842–1292: Succession and Independence* (Edinburgh, 2002), pp. 23–5.
[3] Davies, *First English Empire*, ch. 3.
[4] Davies, 'Names, boundaries and regnal solidarities', 12–13; Lieberman, 'Striving for Marcher liberties: the Corbets'.
[5] R. R. Davies, 'The identity of "Wales" in the thirteenth century', in idem and G. H. Jenkins (eds), *From Medieval to Modern Wales: Historical Essays in Honour of Kenneth O. Morgan and Ralph A. Griffiths* (Cardiff, 2004), pp. 45–63.
[6] W. Lindesay, *The Great Wall* (Oxford, 2003).
[7] J. Wacher (ed.), *The Roman World* (2 vols, London, 1990), vol. 1, pt 4; C. R. Whittaker, *Frontiers of the Roman Empire* (Baltimore, MD, 1994); D. J. Breeze, *The Northern Frontiers of Roman Britain* (London, 1982).
[8] F. J. Turner, *The Frontier in American History* (New York, 1921). For remarks on the relevance of Turner's thesis to the March of Wales, cf. Nelson, *The Normans in South Wales*, esp. pp. 129, 181–4.
[9] Davies, *Age of Conquest*, pp. 3–4.
[10] D. Hill and M. Worthington, *Offa's Dyke: History and Guide* (Stroud, 2003).
[11] Ibid., *passim*; but see the critical review by I. Bapty in *Studia Celtica*, 38 (2004), 201–2.
[12] Pryce, 'British or Welsh?'
[13] Cf. Davies, *Patterns of Power*, p. 67.
[14] J. Campbell, 'The late Anglo-Saxon state: a maximum view', in idem, *The Anglo-Saxon State* (London, 2000), p. 10.
[15] Ibid., pp. 6–7.
[16] A. Williams, 'An introduction to the Worcestershire Domesday', in idem and R. W. H. Erskine (eds), *The Worcestershire Domesday* (Alecto County Edition of Domesday Book, 5, London, 1988), pp. 10–11, 13, 15; C. P. Lewis, 'An introduction to the Herefordshire Domesday', in A. Williams and R. W. H. Erskine (eds), *The Herefordshire Domesday* (Alecto County Edition of Domesday Book, 6, London, 1988), p. 7.
[17] William of Malmesbury, *Gesta regum*, vol. 1, ed. and trans. R. A. B. Mynors, compl. R. M. Thomson and M. Winterbottom (Oxford, 1998), p. 216 (§134.6).
[18] *Orderic*, ed. Chibnall, vi, 520.
[19] Lewis, 'Introduction to the Herefordshire Domesday', p. 7.
[20] Cf. Gerald of Wales, *Journey/Description*, p. 224 (*Description*, i, 4).
[21] 'Mawl Hywel ap Goronwy', ed. R. Geraint Gruffydd, in *Gwaith Meilyr Brydydd a'i Ddysgynyddion*, ed. J. E. Caerwyn Williams and P. I. Lynch (Cardiff, 1994), no. 10, l. 9; cf. Pryce, 'British or Welsh?', 777.
[22] DB 181; Lewis, 'Introduction to the Herefordshire Domesday', pp. 8–9.
[23] DB 179; Davies, 'Bloodfeud'.

[24] DB 268–9; C. P. Lewis, 'An introduction to the Cheshire Domesday', in A. Williams and R. W. H. Erskine (eds), *The Cheshire Domesday* (Alecto County Edition of Domesday Book, 20, London, 1991), pp. 1–25; F. R. Thorn, 'Hundreds and Wapentakes', ibid., pp. 26–44.

[25] Lewis, 'Introduction to Herefordshire Domesday', pp. 8–9.

[26] *Cartae*, i, no. 35.

[27] *Cartae*, i, no. 126, p. 122; ii, no. 523.

[28] For example, Shropshire Archives 552/1/5a, m. 2v: 'Halimot Wallicorum' (1335).

[29] Lloyd, *History of Wales*, pp. 427–8.

[30] *Pipe Roll 31 Henry I*, pp. 136–7.

[31] Ibid., pp. 89–90.

[32] R. R. Davies, 'The English state and the "Celtic" peoples, 1100–1400', *Journal of Historical Sociology*, 6 (1993), 1–14; idem, *First English Empire*, *passim*, esp. pp. 193–201.

[33] *Pipe Roll 31 Henry I*, pp. 142–3.

[34] Holt, *Northerners*, chs 11 and 12.

[35] Gerald of Wales, *Expugnatio Hibernica*, ed. Scott and Martin, pp. 236–7 (ii, 37).

[36] Martin, 'John, lord of Ireland', pp. 143–6; 'The Irish Pipe Roll of 14 John, 1211–12', ed. O. Davies and D. B. Quinn, in *Ulster Journal of Archaeology*, 3rd ser., supplement to vol. 4 (1941). (This is the only surviving Irish pipe roll.)

[37] *Rotuli de oblatis et finibus, tempore regis Johannis*, ed. T. D. Hardy (London, 1835), p. 36.

[38] P. Brand, 'Ireland and the literature of the early common law', *Irish Jurist*, NS, 16/1 (1981), 95–6.

[39] R. Frame, *Colonial Ireland* (Dublin, 1981), ch. 5, 'English institutions'.

[40] Davies, 'Laws and customs'.

[41] Davies, *First English Empire*, p. 160.

[42] The use of the term 'empire' here is suggested by Davies, *First English Empire*.

[43] Gerald of Wales, *Journey/Description*, p. 126 (*Journey*, i, 7).

[44] *Foreign Accounts of Henry III, 1219–34*, ed. F. Cazel (PRS, 44, 1974–5), p. 56; Davies, *Lordship and Society*, p. 17.

[45] *Calendar of Patent Rolls, 1281–92* (London, 1893), p. 419.

[46] *List of Welsh Entries in the Memoranda Rolls, 1282–1343*, ed. N. Fryde (Cardiff, 1974), no. 68.

6

Conclusion: the European Perspective

The March of Wales was only one of the borderlands of the medieval Latin west. Europe had a number of internal frontier regions, such as Lorraine, which was one of the westernmost parts of the Holy Roman Empire. Other borders were more external in nature, notably that between the Christian- and the Muslim-controlled parts of the Iberian peninsula. By the late eighth century, Charlemagne's empire had had 'marches', defensive border commands, one of which was, indeed, called the 'march' of Spain ('marcha Hispanica').[1] The March of Wales can therefore be placed within a Europe-wide context. And there is every reason why it should be. All historical border regions have the potential to illuminate each other by being compared and contrasted. Moreover, there is a specific benefit to focusing on the borderlands of medieval Europe. For if frontiers have much to reveal about the nature of countries, kingdoms, states or empires, then why not continents? Discussing the borders of medieval Europe should in principle shed light on what 'Europe' was during the Middle Ages.[2]

Today, the extensive tract of land which lies to the north of the Ore Mountains, between the rivers Elbe and Oder, is partly in Germany and partly in Poland. It was a true borderland throughout the medieval period. The settlement history of this part of Europe is still not fully understood. The rough picture is that in the very early Middle Ages, Germanic tribes lived here, but that these mostly moved south and west, to be replaced by Slavs. Not all of the land was easy to live in. The area around Berlin, what is now the state of Brandenburg, was characterized by river valleys, which were settled first, but also by higher, relatively arid plateaus such as the Barnim, which remained forested until the later Middle Ages. Moreover, the level coastal regions in the north were rather marshy, dotted with lakes and veined with numerous waterways leading to the North Sea and the Baltic Sea. By 1100, the Slavic settlers here had long been hard at work draining land to gain arable, and building roads and settlements. Foreign observers told of wooden bridges several kilometres long which crossed the many lakes and rivers. There was a considerable amount of trade and craftsmanship, as has been shown by the discovery of tenth- and eleventh-century treasures. Even in 1100, the Slavic population east of the Elbe appears to have been organized in tribes; it had not gelled into a single political entity. It was also pagan. Its pantheon included the club-wielding thunder-god Perun, who was not dissimilar to the Scandinavian god Thor. German and Danish ecclesiastics wrote in horror of the Liutic people, who bore idols of their gods in the vanguard of their armies; of the fire-deity Svarožič, worshipped in the unidentified fortress of Riedegost together with a multitude of other gods and goddesses; and of the temple of the god Svantevit with his four-headed statue, at Arkona, on the island of Rügen in the Baltic Sea.[3]

East of the Elbe, then, medieval Europe was a border zone of religions and of peoples. It was also a military and political frontierland, contested between the king of Germany, the lords of the Carolingian 'marches', or *Marken*, the kings of Poland, pagan Slavic rulers and even, in the north, the Danes. The area around the fortress of Brandenburg was of special strategic importance: it provided access to the system of waterways centred on the Havel and the Spree rivers. Between 928 and 1157, it changed hands no less than thirteen times.[4] Notably, in 983, after the death of Otto II, the king of Germany, Slavic warriors and free peasants combined forces in the 'Liutic alliance' and succeeded in driving the German troops and the bishops of Brandenburg and Havelberg back across the Elbe.

No doubt military antagonism was exacerbated by religious tensions. But by the twelfth century Christian mission was merging with a decidedly profit-oriented approach to attacks on pagans. Thus, in 1108, about ten years after the First Crusade to the Near East, the secular lords and bishops of Saxony, foremost among them Adalgot, archbishop of Magdeburg, added the following afterthought to their appeal for a crusade against the Slavs:

> The pagans are despicable, but their land is rich in meat, honey, flour ... and birds, and if it is cultivated, it brings forth an incomparable bounty of crops ... Therefore, you Saxons, Franks, Lotharingians and Flemings, you famous conquerors of the world, here you may save your souls and, if you so please, obtain splendid land to settle.[5]

Words like this made a lasting impression. In 1147, the Germans of Saxony refused to participate in the Second Crusade to the Near East,

CONCLUSION: THE EUROPEAN PERSPECTIVE

arguing that their responsibility lay in bringing Christianity to their Slavic neighbours. A Saxon crusading army did in fact sweep across the Elbe. But it also laid siege to Stettin in Pomerania, where the townspeople, who had been Christianized in the 1120s, desperately attempted to remind their attackers of that fact by displaying crosses along the city walls. As the chronicler Vincent of Prague wrily observed, 'Deus non fuit in causa': 'God was not at stake'.[6]

In fact, that episode was just a minor incident in an eastwards migratory movement of historic proportions which was just getting under way in the twelfth century. Some of that migration, which is generally referred to by German-speaking historians today as the *Ostsiedlung*, the 'settlement of the east', followed in the wake of military conquests; but its sheer scale suggests it was largely peaceful. It involved peasants, burgesses and monks, mainly from Germany, but also from other western European countries, such as the Netherlands. By *c.*1400, these migrants had settled everywhere between Elbe and Oder, and put down roots beyond the river Weichsel in what is now north-eastern Poland; indeed, some had been carried beyond the kingdom of Hungary as far as what is today Romania. No military campaigns commensurate with this vast migratory movement ever took place.[7]

On the other hand, here and there, military campaigns certainly played a role. One of the participants in the 1147 'crusade' against the Slavs was known as Albrecht (Albert) the Bear. The scion of an old Saxon noble family, the Ascanians, he had joined forces with the bishop of Magdeburg, leading an army from that town across the Elbe and capturing Havelberg. But his greatest success came ten years later, when he managed to take the Brandenburg, a very well-sited fortification situated on an island in the river Havel. In the wake of this military milestone followed the gradual but lasting Christianization of the populace. The first step was destroying the idol in the temple of Brandenburg and reactivating the bishopric. But economic considerations were evidently close to Albert's heart too. In 1157, the same year he conquered the Brandenburg, we are told he sent out for Dutchmen, Zeelanders and Flemings, 'those who live by the ocean and suffered the might of the sea', and began to settle them 'in the towns and villages of the Slavs'.[8] In the case of what came to be known as the *Mark* of Brandenburg, the path for the *Ostsiedlung* was certainly cleared by the sword.

The retreat of pagan Slav power in the second half of the twelfth century was not limited to the *Mark* of Brandenburg. In 1168, after a siege lasting several weeks, the temple at Arkona was destroyed by a

Danish army which forced the populace to yield up the statue of the god Svantevit along with the temple treasure.[9] But the *Mark* of Brandenburg provides a particularly illuminating example, since it reveals the mechanics of how military domination and agricultural colonization was extended eastwards.[10] The process was only set in motion by Albert the Bear, who died in 1170. It took decades. But it remained in the family. It proceeded under the auspices of his descendants, the later Ascanians, who were margraves of Brandenburg until their dynasty, which numbered nineteen males in *c.*1290, came to an unexpected and not yet satisfactorily explained end in 1319. By that time, however, the *Mark* had been extended about 200 kilometres east of the Elbe, all the way to the Oder. From 1231, the Slavic dukes of Pomerania, to the east of the Oder, owed them fealty as well.

The task of expanding the *Mark* of Brandenburg was not always personally undertaken by the Ascanian margraves; but they kept a close eye on things. Probably all the men on the ground owed their allegiance to them. Many of them had been associated with them before the conquest of the Brandenburg; others were recruited to their service afterwards. Some came from the old Ascanian lordships between the Harz mountains and the Elbe, the *Altmark* or 'old *Mark*' – the von Kerkow family, for instance, who are named from Kerkau, a town just to the west of the Elbe. Other families made greater journeys in their quest for fortune. The von Wedels, who entered the service of the dukes of Pomerania in the thirteenth century, came from Holstein, just to the south of Denmark. They settled east of the Oder and by the later thirteenth century had divided their loyalties between the dukes of Pomerania and the Ascanians. Not all of the knightly settlers are as well known. Often their activities can only be discerned through the evidence of place-names. Thus, the Brandenburg village of Blocksdorf, 'Block's village', was owned by the family of that name in 1298, and it is probable that this family also founded Blockshagen.[11] Baldwin, one of the margraves' 'ministerials', or unfree knights, almost certainly established the village of Bollersdorf in the Barnim: it is spelled 'Boldewinstorff' in the sources.[12] Even the activities of the von Wedels are often only revealed through toponyms. Clearly that family was particularly active in the *Neumark*, the lands beyond the Oder which came under Ascanian control in the thirteenth century. Von Wedels are commemorated in the place-names of Wedelsdorf, Hassendorf, Zühlshagen, Zühlsdorf and Lämersdorf.[13]

Almost invariably, these knightly pioneers relied on building castles to underpin their power. The initiative for economic development, too, lay largely in their hands. In 1313, Ludolf the Elder von Wedel sold the village of Venzlaffshagen to a pair of knightly brothers and promised them sixty-four additional hides of land if they undertook to found further settlements. Once these lands were profitable, the brothers were to provide the military service of a fully armoured warhorse.[14] Enterprising individuals acted as *locatores*, accepting the responsibility of developing a stretch of land in return for a share in the profits.[15] In a thinly populated country, the new villages were generally inhabited by immigrant Germans; some villages had a mixed population, and a very few were entirely Slavic. Evidence for the displacement of the Slavic population of the *Mark* is rare. In 1245, the bishop of Halberstadt granted the monks of the abbey of Diesdorf permission to evict any Slavs on their land who refused to abstain from pagan rites.[16] There is one documented case of forcible removal of Slavs in the Brandenburg. In 1273, the margraves permitted the Cistercians of Mariensee abbey to move to Chorin and granted them the Slavic village of Rogäsen. A charter of bishop Heinrich von Brandenburg of the following year shows that the Slavic villagers had by that time been evicted.[17] On the other hand, the higher ground near Berlin, Barnim and Teltow, where there had been no settlements in the early twelfth century, was asserted during the twelfth and thirteenth centuries with much participation by Slavic peasants.

The more substantial urban foundations were the prerogative of the lords of Brandenburg themselves. Berlin received the privileges of Brandenburg, around 1230, from John I and Otto III, the pair of brothers who jointly ruled the *Mark* at the time. Towns were also established further east, in what is now Poland. One such frontier town was Deutsch Krone (now Wałcz). Here, the margraves' charter of 1303 shows that the town was part of a larger strategy to fortify an exposed frontier region. Two knights, Ulrich of Schöning and Rudolf of Liebenthal, were employed as *locatores*, each receiving 320 hides, enough to establish five villages of sixty-four hides each. They were freed from service to the margraves for sixteen years. The same deal, sixty-four hides free of service for sixteen years, was offered to any of their knightly friends who could be persuaded to accept.[18]

The creation of the Ascanian lordship of Brandenburg was paralleled, over a thousand kilometres to the west, in Ireland. Here, a colonial aristocracy was advancing into an anciently Christianized country. Nevertheless, its methods were clearly akin to those employed by Albert the Bear and his descendants. Indeed, Hugh de Lacy, to whom Henry II had prospectively granted the Irish kingdom of Meath in 1172, was apparently particularly fond of erecting his mottes within the precincts of Irish ecclesiastical sites.[19] Other English barons in Ireland continued to launch conquests after Henry II's intervention in 1171–2: in Ulster, John de Courcy, who was probably a knight from Somerset; in Leinster, Theobald Walter or Butler. As has been seen, there seems to have been a settlement vacuum in the Irish provinces first occupied, in Leinster, Meath and Ulster, which attracted significant peasant settlement from other parts of Ireland, but also from Britain, notably from the March of Wales.[20] Urban life was already burgeoning in Ireland by the days of Diarmait Mac Murchada, Strongbow and Henry II. Dublin, Waterford and Wexford were all old Viking strongholds which had become permanent bases and thrived on looting. By the twelfth century they had become centres for international trade between the Scandinavian north and the Mediterranean.[21] But it was the English who brought the liberties of Breteuil to Ireland, and only then did urban foundations multiply.

Thus, in the twelfth and thirteenth centuries, very similar projects of conquest and colonization were under way in an anciently Christianized part of the British Isles and in a pagan territory to the east of the Elbe. Building castles and installing deputies by giving them an interest in the land may seem a natural way of securing a conquest territory. However, if it is not accepted that the similarities were simply due to coincidence, then they demand a different explanation. Professor Robert Bartlett has provided one. In a widely read and much-debated book, he proposed that the establishment of the *Mark* of Brandenburg and of lordships in Ireland were not separate, but part of the same process, one he termed the 'Europeanization of Europe'. Thus, his explanation for the broad but undeniable similarities between the marches in Ireland and the *Mark* of Brandenburg was that they reveal the expansion of a vast but increasingly homogeneous cultural area which it makes sense to call 'Europe'. This expansion and internal cultural assimilation was not, of course, centrally coordinated. Rather, the similarities between the two fringes, Ireland and Brandenburg, show the success of certain cultural blueprints, or forms, which originated in the heartlands of Europe – to wit, the former Carolingian empire – but which travelled outwards from there. They were carried by conquering aristocracies; they were conveyed non-violently, and more slowly, by migration of peasants, burgesses and monks; and they spread through acculturation, that is, borrowing between neighbouring cultures or societies.

The forms or blueprints which lent themselves most readily to such cultural transfer were legal concepts such as the chartered borough.

Between c.1100 and c.1300, newly founded towns with remarkably similar urban privileges were established everywhere from Seville to Stockholm and from Galway to Berlin, and the resulting long-distance trade fostered economic and cultural exchange at unprecedented levels. Villages, too, were set up and granted privileges wherever arable was being won by assarting or by the draining of marshes. Agricultural technology and practices, particularly those geared towards increasing cereal production, followed in the wake of settlers or were imitated by native populations: the mill, that 'biggest machine of the medieval world', and new and improved kinds of plough. Other traces of this high medieval Europeanization are manifold. Members of the aristocracies began to draw their first names from a common, fairly limited stock of favourites – such as, famously, William. While earlier medieval European society had been fiercely devoted to its local saints, cults for 'national', even 'international' saints now became the fashion, particularly of the apostles Peter and John, of the Mother of God, and of God himself. Coinages, modelled on Charlemagne's and on those of the Anglo-Saxon kings, began to replace barter systems. The practice of using a particular type of written instrument, the charter, for conveying land or recording grants similarly spread outwards from Carolingian Francia.[22]

These elements undeniably demarcated a great cultural sphere, whether or not it is labelled 'Europe'. If that label is accepted, however, then high medieval Europe was not Latin Christendom.[23] True, as the 'new Europe' advanced into pagan Slav territory east of the Elbe, bishoprics were established, or rather re-established, in its wake. But the case of Ireland shows that this Europe also divided Christianized countries whose church had recognized the supremacy of the pope. Or take Poland. Christianity had reached Poland from the west (rather than from Byzantium) in the tenth century, when the first Polish king to be baptized founded the bishopric of Poznán. However, Polish territory was only belatedly, gradually, and indeed incompletely 'Europeanized'. Foreign, mainly German, peasants and burgesses did encroach upon it from the west, and settled in newly established villages and towns on the legal terms familiar to them from their homelands. But the kingdom of Poland, like Ireland, was only partly 'Europeanized' in this way during the high Middle Ages. Both countries were Christian. But neither was completely integrated into the high medieval 'Europe' identified by Bartlett. It is this insight which makes his book far more than a synthesis. That high medieval growth and expansion was a Europe-wide phenomenon had of course been noticed before. But it was Bartlett who gave due emphasis to the view that the advance of the 'new' Europe, as it had defined itself by c.1300, was not equivalent to the advance of Christianity. What he called the high medieval 'Europeanization of Europe' added a further cultural layer, and new cultural frontiers, to the Latin west. These were not everywhere coterminous with the old ones. At the same time, the newly Europeanized Europe gave rise to novel perceptions of civilization, which clerical spokesmen within the 'new' Europe equated with Christianity. It is this which explains how they could describe the Irish as 'Christians in name, pagans in fact'.[24]

Wherever one chooses to stand on the issue of medieval 'Europeanization', the debate is clearly relevant to the March of Wales. The March may have been a unique phenomenon in the British Isles. But that is not to deny that some of its features were shared by the other boundary of England, to wit, the border with Scotland. Nor is it to exclude the possibility that both may have had parallels with the marches between the Irish- and English-settled parts of Ireland. It follows that there is a case for seeing the March of Wales not only as a borderland of medieval Britain, but of medieval Europe.

It is true that in the case of the March, and indeed of Ireland and Scotland too, there is a complication. This arises because of the ambiguous status of England. In the first place, England had a highly developed sense of cultural and political distinctiveness before 1066. Moreover, after 1066, England itself became colonized. Further, it continued to develop distinctively English features even after 1066 (particularly, but not only, in the realm of law and government). As a result, the influence exerted by medieval England on the rest of the British Isles combined old Anglo-Saxon elements, 'European' features and post-1066 English innovations. Thus, many of the features of the main medieval colonizing movement in the British Isles were arguably not 'European', but quintessentially English. In the context of the British Isles, therefore, the Europeanization of England and its Celtic neighbours can be distinguished, conceptually at least, from the Anglicization of Scotland, Wales and Ireland.

Arguably, the history of the March of Wales shows that the two were inextricably intertwined. Glamorgan reveals this clearly. The imposition of military control here proceeded by encastellation and subinfeudation, those staples of the high medieval expansion of Europe which were essential ingredients of the *Mark* of Brandenburg and of the English lordships in Ireland. But in Glamorgan, as has been noted, the building of castles and the creation of knights' fees went hand in glove with the

CONCLUSION: THE EUROPEAN PERSPECTIVE

establishment of a new 'shire', albeit one designed to serve the lord at Cardiff rather than the king of England. There is much to be said for the view that the shire itself was a cultural blueprint admirably suited for export, like the chartered borough or coinages.[25] Henry I, as has been seen, had both a sheriff and a mint at Pembroke.[26] Establishing shires was one of the first things Henry II did in Ireland in 1171–2, and it was a similar priority for Edward I in *pura Wallia* after 1282–3. What is more, the kings of Scotland were just as quick off the mark as the Norman and Plantagenet kings of England. The work of organizing royal demesne along the lines of the English shire had been begun by David I.[27] By *c.*1300 there were some twenty-six shires in Scotland. But there was nothing European about shires whatsoever. They certainly were not to be found in the *Mark* of Brandenburg. The same point could be made about other English institutions which were reproduced in a Scottish context, such as the justices in ayre (as justices in eyre were known in Scotland), or certain features of the common law.[28] There is scope for debate on how far the countries adjoining high medieval England were Anglicized, rather than Europeanized.

But perhaps to separate Europeanization and Anglicization too strictly would be artificial. In the British Isles, England was undoubtedly a complicating factor which has to be borne in mind. On the other fringes of high medieval 'Europe', in Spain, say, or in Sicily, or in Scandinavia, other complicating factors lent local colour to the 'Europeanization of Europe'. Nevertheless, a challenging and interesting question remains. There is certainly a dimension to the March which only becomes apparent once a very wide context is taken into consideration. There is an opportunity to discuss what the making of the March tells us about the making of Europe.

All the elements are there. The same colonial aristocracy that overran England and swept into Ireland entrenched itself along the Welsh borders and in south Wales.[29] Indeed, the March acted as a relay for the incursions into Ireland, since those incursions were initiated by the descendants of the first Norman conquerors in south Wales. Moreover, there can be no doubt that, in many cases, successive generations of peasant and burgess settlers leapfrogged from England to Ireland by way of the March. Both in the March and in Ireland, there was a close link between military conquest, underpinned by the construction of mottes, and the immigration of rural and urban settlers, encouraged by the colonial lords. In some parts of the March, certainly in the south, the distinction between immigrant and native populations was slowly reinforced by a lowland–upland divide and probably also a difference in emphasis in economic practice. The foreign-settled coastal areas subsisted on a predominantly, though by no means exclusively, arable economy, in keeping with the high value placed on wheat by northern French and much of English society at the time. The idealization of arable may explain the bemusement with which authors like Gerald of Wales regarded mixed arable–pastoral societies like those of native Wales. As has been seen, in his case this may have been reinforced by a division of land and labour along ethnic lines in the south of Wales.[30] But again it is important to note that some of the elements of the standardized image of the Welsh – and the Irish – that he painted were paralleled by authors on the pagan frontier in eastern Europe. To the colonists in the *Ostsiedlung* contrasts in economic practices were as striking as the religious difference. This similarity in outlook is yet another element which reveals the 'European' dimension of the March of Wales.[31]

In both Ireland and Wales, too, deeply different societies met, lived within sight of each other, intermingled and needed to adapt to the challenges this entailed.[32] As a result, it could be argued that the legal and institutional arrangements enshrined in Welshries and Englishries and in the laws of the March must be seen in a European context as well.[33] If so, the manorial courts in the *Ostsiedlung* which applied Polish or German law depending on the nationality of litigants are more than comparative evidence. They show that frontier territories such as the *Mark* of Brandenburg and the March of Wales were caught up in the same, contemporary historical process. That argument is substantiated by the fact that the March was also a borderland of languages and of customs, not least conventions in warfare. What is more, it may well be that the beginnings of the ethnic exclusivity of the English 'state', which is paralleled by a deterioration in relations between peoples throughout later medieval Europe,[34] is reflected in the interactions between agents of the English 'state' and Welsh-populated parts of the March.

The European dimension certainly survived throughout the first phase of Marcher history. The Stradlings, a knightly family which established itself in Glamorgan during Edward I's reign, came from Strättlingen on the lake of Thun, in what is now the Bernese canton of Switzerland.[35] But after 1300, as the pressure on land in the March ebbed away due to the hunger and plague catastrophes in England and abroad, and as the March lost its military *raison d'être*, its character as a 'European' borderland probably decreased. In any case, this seems likely to have been the case in comparison to Ireland, where the English lordship increasingly came under siege, in a military and cultural sense, as the

Middle Ages progressed.[36] Nevertheless, even in the fourteenth century the March remained a social and cultural borderland; and the fifteenth century opened with the revolt of Owain Glyn Dŵr.[37] Perhaps there is a case for considering the later history of the March in a 'European' context too.

Such are some of the questions to which Marcher studies will contribute answers. The March of Wales, and particularly the first two centuries of its history, promises to reveal facts about high medieval colonialism in all its facets: the mechanics and transfer of military technology (particularly the castle); and the progress of high medieval migratory movements that had a lasting impact on the linguistic and cultural map of Britain. Moreover, studying the March will lead to discoveries about the cultural rifts between the different societies in the British Isles. Few regions are better suited to investigating how deep those rifts were, how they developed and how they were perceived, at a time when the identities of the Welsh and of the English were going through a critical phase. Future studies on medieval 'states', too, will benefit from devoting attention to the March. It is not just that the March impinges very directly on the history of the most advanced of all the 'states' of high medieval Europe. The Marcher lordships, themselves highly autonomous territories with their own jurisdictional and administrative structures, challenge medieval historians to rethink how they deploy the concept of 'the state'.[38] The medieval March is also a showcase for observing the processes of cultural transfer and confrontation which accompanied the high medieval 'Europeanization of Europe'. These are, let it be stressed again, just some possible avenues and perspectives that might profitably be pursued in depth. There is absolutely no doubt that there are others. All the more reason to hope and expect that Marcher studies will continue to flourish.

Notes

[1] *Vita Hludowici imperatoris*, ed. G. H. Pertz, in *Monumenta Germaniae Historica, Scriptores*, 2 (Hanover, 1829), ch. 42, p. 631; cf. J. Dhondt, 'Le titre du marquis à l'époque carolingienne', *Archivum Latinitatis Medii Aevi (Bulletin Du Cange)*, 19 (1948), 407–17.
[2] Cf. Bartlett, *Making of Europe*.

[3] Thietmar von Merseburg, *Chronik*, ed. and trans. W. Trillmich (Freiherr vom Stein-Gedächtnisausgabe, 9, Berlin, 1960), pp. 266–9; *Die Chronik des Bischofs Thietmar von Merseburg und ihre Korveier Überarbeitung*, ed. R. Holtzmann, in *Monumenta Germaniae Historica, Scriptores rerum Germanicarum*, ns, 9 (Berlin, 1935), pp. 301–2 (vi, 22–3); Helmold von Bosau, *Helmolds Slavenchronik*, ed. B. Schmeidler, in *Monumenta Germaniae Historica, Scriptores rerum Germanicum in usum scholarum separatim editi*, 32 (Hanover, 1937), p. 214; Saxo Grammaticus, *Saxonis gesta Danorum*, ed. J. Olrik and H. Ræder (2 vols, Copenhagen, 1931–57), i, 464–73 (bk 14, ch. 19, §§1–34).

[4] J. Herrmann (ed.), *Die Slawen in Deutschland* (Berlin, 1985), p. 398.

[5] *Urkunden und erzählende Quellen zur deutschen Ostsiedlung im Mittelalter*, ed. H. Helbig and L. Weinrich (2 vols, Darmstadt, 1968), i, 102–3.

[6] *Vincenti Pragensis annales*, ed. W. Wattenbach, in *Monumenta Germaniae Historica, Scriptores*, 17 (Hanover, 1861), p. 663.

[7] W. Schlesinger (ed.), *Die deutsche Ostsiedlung des Mittelalters als Problem der europäischen Geschichte: Reichenau-Vorträge 1970–1972* (Sigmaringen, 1975).

[8] Helmold, ed. Schmeidler, pp. 174–5 (bk 1, ch. 89); cf. H. K. Schulze, 'Die Besiedlung der Mark Brandenburg im hohen und späten Mittelalter', *Jahrbuch für die Geschichte Ost- und Mitteldeutschlands*, 28 (1979), 123: linguistic studies suggest that settlers actually came from the Rhine delta, Flanders and Brabant, but not from coastal areas.

[9] Helmold, ed. Schmeidler, pp. 214–17 (bk 2, chs 108–9).

[10] Bartlett, *Making of Europe*, pp. 33–9.

[11] Schulze, 'Brandenburg', 120.

[12] Ibid., p. 118.

[13] Ibid., p. 116.

[14] Ibid., p. 120.

[15] Bartlett, *Making of Europe*, pp. 121–2.

[16] Schulze, 'Brandenburg', 124–5.

[17] Ibid., p. 125.

[18] Ibid., p. 120.

[19] B. J. Graham, 'The mottes of the Norman liberty of Meath', in H. Murtagh (ed.), *Irish Midland Studies: Essays in Commemoration of N. W. English* (Athlone, 1980), p. 29.

[20] Above, Ch. 3.

[21] R. E. Glasscock, 'Land and people, *c.*1300', in A. Cosgrove (ed.), *New History of Ireland*, vol. 2 (Oxford, 1987), p. 234.

[22] Bartlett, *Making of Europe*, ch. 7 (towns and trade); ch. 5 (villages); ch. 6 (cereal-growing technology; p. 143 for quotation about the mill); pp. 270–4 (saints); pp. 180–3 (coins and charters).

[23] Cf. ibid., p. 21.

[24] Ibid., p. 22, quoting St Bernard of Clairvaux, *Vita sancti Malachiae*, 8, 16.

[25] Davies, *First English Empire*, pp. 165–6.

[26] *Pipe Roll 31 Henry I*, pp. 136–7.

[27] Duncan, *Scotland*, pp. 161–3, 596–7.

CONCLUSION: THE EUROPEAN PERSPECTIVE

[28] *Atlas of Scottish History*, p. 187; H. MacQueen, 'Scots law under Alexander III', in N. H. Reid (ed.), *Scotland in the Reign of Alexander III, 1249–1286* (Edinburgh, 1990), esp. pp. 92–5.
[29] For the term cf. R. Bartlett, 'Colonial aristocracies', in Bartlett and MacKay (eds), *Medieval Frontier Societies*, pp. 23–47.
[30] Pryce, 'Deheubarth', 272.
[31] Bartlett, *Gerald of Wales*, ch. 6.
[32] R. R. Davies, 'Frontier arrangements in fragmented societies: Ireland and Wales', in Bartlett and MacKay (eds), *Medieval Frontier Societies*, pp. 77–100.
[33] Bartlett, *Making of Europe*, ch. 8.
[34] Ibid., pp. 236–42.
[35] R. A. Griffiths, 'John de Estratlinges (d. *c.*1293)', in *ODNB*.
[36] Cf. Davies, *First English Empire*, ch. 7, 'The ebb tide of the English empire, 1304–1343'.
[37] Davies, *Lordship and Society*, *passim*; idem, *The Revolt of Owain Glyn Dŵr* (Oxford, 1995).
[38] R. R. Davies, 'The medieval state: the tyranny of a concept?', *Journal of Historical Sociology*, 16 (2003), 280–99.

Key Dates

1050 (c.)	Normans build castles on Welsh borders (Hereford, Richard's Castle and Ewyas Harold)
1063	Gruffudd ap Llywelyn, king of Gwynedd and of Deheubarth, killed
1066	Harold, king of England, achieves victories over Vikings at Fulford and Stamford Bridge, but is defeated by William of Normandy at Hastings
1067–71	William fitz Osbern, earl in Wessex and lord of Hereford, builds and rebuilds castles on south-eastern Welsh border, including Chepstow, Ewyas Lacy and Wigmore
1070s	The earl of Shrewsbury, Roger de Montgomery, and his sons lead raids into Wales; so does Hugh d'Avranches (the Fat), the earl of Chester
1075	Roger de Breteuil, son of William fitz Osbern, rebels; forfeits earldom of Hereford
1081	William I of England travels to St David's
1086	Domesday Book mentions a 'March of Wales'
1093	Rhys ap Tewdwr, king of Deheubarth, killed; Norman raids into Wales intensify
1094	Effective wave of Welsh counterattacks
1095	William II's first Welsh campaign
1096	Further Welsh counterattacks
1097	William II's second Welsh campaign
1100	Death of William II of England; accession of Henry I
1102	Robert of Bellême rebels; forfeits the earldom of Shrewsbury; English crown is by far the largest landholder in the border county of Shropshire
1110	Gilbert fitz Richard de Clare and his men undertake the conquest of Ceredigion
1114	Henry I's first Welsh campaign

1121	Henry I's second Welsh campaign
1135	Henry I dies; accession of Stephen to throne of England
1136–8	The sons of Gruffudd ap Cynan destroy Clare castles in Ceredigion
1140s	Lords of central Welsh borders at war with Welsh rulers of Elfael and Maelienydd
1149	Madog ap Maredudd in possession of Oswestry castle
1154	Death of Stephen; accession of Henry II
1157	Henry II leads a campaign against Deheubarth
1158	Henry II leads a campaign against Gwynedd
1160	Death of Madog ap Maredudd, ruler of Powys
1165	Henry II leads a failed campaign against united Welsh army encamped in Powys
1166	References to a 'March' and a 'March of Wales' begin to appear in the Pipe Rolls
1167	Invasion of Ireland commences; détente in the March begins, no English king invades Wales until 1211
1170	Death of Owain Gwynedd
1170s and 1180s	Numerous Marcher dynasties die out in the male line, including Clare earls of Pembroke, Beaumont of Gower, earls of Gloucester (lords of Glamorgan)
1171–2	Henry II in Ireland, concludes truces with rulers in Wales on way there and back
1175, 1177	Henry II's councils with Welsh princes including the Lord Rhys of Deheubarth and Dafydd of Gwynedd
1188	Gerald of Wales journeys around Wales preaching the Third Crusade
1189	Death of Henry II; accession of Richard I
1196	The Lord Rhys defeats Roger Mortimer of Wigmore
1199	Death of Richard I; accession of John; William de Braose, lord of Abergavenny, Brecon, Builth, Elfael and Radnor, declares that the king's writ does not run in his Marcher lordships
1203	Fulk Fitzwarin III of Whittington outlawed by John of England
1204–5	John of England loses Normandy and most of his other Continental lands in wars with Philip Augustus, the king of France
1208	John orders the arrest of the Braoses

KEY DATES

1211, 1212	John's Welsh campaigns
1213	Llywelyn ab Iorwerth conquers the Perfeddwlad
1215	Llywelyn ab Iorwerth occupies Shrewsbury; Magna Carta mentions the 'law of the March'
1216	Death of John; accession of 9-year-old Henry III
1218	Treaty of Worcester; Llywelyn ab Iorwerth is confirmed in his conquests, receives provisional custody of Cardigan and Carmarthen castles
1219–32	Henry III's justiciar, Hubert de Burgh, earl of Kent, accumulates castles and lordships in south Wales, along with Threecastles and Montgomery, then falls from royal favour
1223	English forces take back from Llywelyn ab Iorwerth the key castles of Carmarthen, Cardigan and Cilgerran, where William Marshal begins to build a masonry castle; the young Henry III of England relieves Builth and builds a new castle at Montgomery
1228	Henry III and Hubert de Burgh lead a bungled raid on Ceri
1230s and 1240s	Numerous Marcher dynasties die out in the male line, including Braose, Lacy, Marshal, fitz Baderon of Monmouth and Clifford
1231	Llywelyn ab Iorwerth again raids castles in the Welsh borders and in south Wales; Henry III leads an ineffectual campaign against him, fortifies Painscastle
1233	Llywelyn ab Iorwerth raids castles in the Welsh borders and in south Wales
1233–4	Richard Marshal, sixth earl of Pembroke, rebels; joins forces with Llywelyn ab Iorwerth, burns Shrewsbury
1234–5	Gilbert Marshal, seventh earl of Pembroke, receives custody of Carmarthen and Cardigan castles as well as of Glamorgan and the Braose estates
1237–41	English crown annexes the county of Cheshire
1240	Death of Llywelyn ab Iorwerth; Walter Marshal raids Ceredigion; beginning of period of ascendancy of English king over Wales
1241	Dafydd, son and heir of Llywelyn ab Iorwerth, forced to submit to Henry III
1244–5	Death of Gruffudd ab Iorwerth ap Llywelyn in 1244; Welsh revolt

1245	Extinction of Marshal dynasty
1246	Death of Dafydd ap Llywelyn
1247	Treaty of Woodstock; the Perfeddwlad conceded to Henry III
1255	Llywelyn ap Gruffudd wins mastery over his brothers at the battle of Bryn Derwin
1256	Llywelyn ap Gruffudd seizes the Perfeddwlad from the English
1258–62	Truce between Llywelyn ap Gruffudd and Henry III as the latter struggles to avoid civil war in England
1262–5	Baronial wars in England; Llywelyn ap Gruffudd supports baronial faction; Mortimer of Wigmore is royalist
1266–7	Conflicts over Disinherited in England prevents English campaign against Llywelyn ap Gruffudd
1267	Treaty of Montgomery: Henry III concedes the Perfeddwlad, Whittington, Ceri, Cedewain, Builth, Gwerthrynion and Brycheinog to Llywelyn ap Gruffudd, who is titled 'prince of Wales'
1268	Earl Gilbert de Clare, lord of Glamorgan, begins work on great masonry castle at Caerffili to consolidate his direct rule over upland commote of Senghennydd
1272	Accession of Edward I of England
1273	Llywelyn ap Gruffudd starts building Dolforwyn castle
1274–6	Relations between Llywelyn and Edward deteriorate, chiefly because of tensions in the March
1276–7	Edward I campaigns in Wales; Llywelyn ap Gruffudd is forced to accept terms (Treaty of Aberconway); Edward begins work on castles at Flint, Rhuddlan, Aberystwyth and Builth
1278–82	Tensions rise between Edward I and Llywelyn as Edward adjudges dispute between Llywelyn and Gruffudd ap Gwenwynwyn over the *cantref* of Arwystli
1281	Agreement between Llywelyn and Roger Mortimer of Wigmore
1282–3	Welsh rebellion erupts in March 1282; Llywelyn ap Gruffudd and Dafydd ap Gruffudd killed in the ensuing wars against Edward I
1284	Edward I's Statute of Rhuddlan; creation of the Principality's shires of Flint, Anglesey, Caernarvon, Merioneth and Cardigan
1291	Edward I is granted Welsh tax
1294–5	Welsh revolt

KEY DATES

1301	Edward, son of Edward II, is created first English prince of Wales
1307	Death of Edward I; accession of Edward II
1536 and 1542	Acts of Union of England and Wales; the Marcher lordships are incorporated into new shires or added to old border counties.

Bibliography

This bibliography lists the sources and works cited in this book. The following brief notes aim to provide thematic guidance.

Chapter 1. Introduction

Chapter 1, in its second, historiographical part, provides some thematic guidance to the works it cites. Frame, *Political Development*, contains valuable historiographical essays. For introductions to the March of Wales, cf. Reeves, *The Marcher Lords*, and Walker, *The Norman Conquerors*. R. R. Davies, *Lordship and Society in the March of Wales* is a milestone in historical writing on the March. W. Rees's remarkable maps of south Wales and the border in the fourteenth century are unsurpassed. For the debate on Marcher liberties see especially George Owen of Henllys (listed among the printed primary sources), J. G. Edwards, 'The Normans and the Welsh March', R. R. Davies, 'Kings, lords and liberties', and the forthcoming volume edited by M. Prestwich on *Liberties and Identities*. R. R. Davies distilled his groundbreaking contribution to the history of the British Isles in his *First English Empire*.

Chapter 2. The Making of the March, 1066–1283

The classic narrative account in Lloyd, *History of Wales*, is magisterially complemented and updated by R. R. Davies, *Age of Conquest*. For the making of the March, *c*.1067 to 1300, cf. especially chapters 4 and 10 in Davies, *Age of Conquest*. I. W. Rowlands, 'The making of the March' and J. B. Smith, 'The kingdom of Morgannwg', are important case-studies focusing respectively on Dyfed and Glamorgan. For general surveys of the conquest aristocracies of the high Middle Ages, see Frame, *Political Development*, ch. 3, and R. Bartlett, *Making of Europe*, ch. 2. On the castles of Wales and the March, cf. especially the important surveys by Hogg and King in *Archaeologia Cambrensis*, and more recently Higham and Barker, *Hen Domen Montgomery*, and the excellent RCAHMW volumes on Glamorgan. On the Welsh borders in the eleventh century see the work of C. P. Lewis. On the ecclesiastical history of the March cf. John Reuben Davies's book and articles. For Ireland during this period cf. the works by Frame, and Cosgrove (ed.), *New History of Ireland*, vol. 2. For the Marchers in Ireland see also Flanagan, *Irish Society, Anglo-Norman Settlers, Angevin Kingship*; Orpen's notes to *The Song of Dermot and the Earl*; and Gerald of Wales, *Expugnatio Hibernica*, ed. Scott and Martin.

Chapter 3. The Social and Economic March, 1067–1300

Dyer, *Making a Living*, provides an excellent and readable introduction to the social and economic history of medieval Britain. It includes a guide to further reading. The volumes in the *Agrarian History of England and Wales*, ed. Thirsk and Miller, cover the high and later Middle Ages. Bartlett, *The Making of Europe*, chapters 5–7, surveys the Continental context. For Wales and the March more particularly, see especially Davies, *Age of Conquest*, chapter 6, Pryce, 'In search of a medieval society', and the relevant chapters in the county histories. On towns, R. A. Griffiths, 'Wales and the marches', in the *Cambridge Urban History of Britain*, provides a useful recent survey. B. G. Charles and G. O. Pierce place the specialist subject of place-name studies in the context of immigration into the March. On the Cistercians in Wales see the work of D. H. Williams.

Chapter 4. The Frontier of Peoples, 1067–1300

On the shaping of the 'ethnic' identities of Britain, see the works cited in the chapter's first paragraph: for the 'English', Wormald and Foot; for the 'Welsh', H. Pryce, 'British or Welsh?'; for the 'Scots', Broun; for a recent general contribution, Charles-Edwards, 'The making of nations in Britain and Ireland'. The identities of the 'English' and of the 'Normans' in England during the twelfth century is a much-debated subject. For two recent differing views see Gillingham, *The English in the Twelfth Century*, and Thomas, *The English and the Normans*. As for the study of chivalry and warfare in high medieval Britain and northern France, this has recently been transformed by the work of Gillingham and of Strickland. In geographical terms, Strickland's focus lies on

BIBLIOGRAPHY   113

England, Scotland and northern France. Gillingham considers England in particular in his '1066', and the British Isles more generally in the articles 'Conquering the barbarians' and 'Killing and mutilating'. For a recent work on warfare in Wales and the March that takes the Welsh evidence even more fully into account cf. Davies, *Welsh Military Institutions*. Crouch, *The Image of Aristocracy*, discusses aristocratic material culture in England, Wales and Scotland. The authority on Welsh heraldry is Siddons.

Chapter 5. Kingdoms, Countries and Marches: the Context of the British Isles

For the state of the debate on Offa's Dyke cf. Hill and Worthington and Bapty's review. Campbell, *Anglo-Saxon State*, powerfully makes the case implied in its title, for seeing the eleventh-century kingdom of England as a state. On early medieval 'Wales', cf. Lloyd, *History of Wales*, Davies, *Patterns of Power*, and the forthcoming volume by Charles-Edwards in the Oxford History of Wales series. On the Welsh borders in the eleventh century, cf. the doctoral thesis, listed articles and forthcoming work by C. P. Lewis. On the medieval English 'state' and its relationship with its Celtic neighbours see R. R. Davies, *First English Empire*, especially chapters 3, 6, and 7, which develop the argument in his 'The English state'.

Chapter 6. Conclusion: the European Perspective

The 'Europeanization of Europe' during the high Middle Ages is traced in a revolutionary way in Bartlett, *Making of Europe*. For a survey of the 'Anglicization of the British Isles', cf. R. R. Davies, *First English Empire*, chapter 6. Lieberman, 'Anglicization in high medieval Wales', is a recent case-study bearing on the March of Wales.

Manuscript and Archival Sources

Chancery, inquisitions *post mortem*: PRO/TNA C 132/35 (18)
Exchequer: Lord Treasurer's Remembrancer: Memoranda Rolls: PRO/TNA E 368/24
Court rolls of Clun lordship: Shropshire Archives 552/1/5a
Survey of Michaelston-le-Pit manor, 1307: Somerset Record Office, DD/WO 47/1

Printed Primary Sources

The Acts of King Stephen, etc., by Richard of Hexham, in *The Priory of Hexham, its Chroniclers, Endowments and Annals*, ed. J. Raine (2 vols, Durham, 1868), i, 63–106.

The Acts of Welsh Rulers, 1120–1283, ed. H. Pryce, ass. C. Insley (Cardiff, 2005).

'The Anglo-Norman chronicle of Wigmore abbey', ed. J. C. Dickinson and P. T. Ricketts, *Transactions of the Woolhope Naturalists' Field Club*, 39 (1969), 413–35.

Annales Cambrie, ed. J. Williams ab Ithel (RS, 1860).

The Autobiography of Gerald of Wales, ed. and trans. H. E. Butler (London, 1937).

Bede's Ecclesiastical History of the English People, ed. B. Colgrave and R. A. B. Mynors (Oxford, 1969).

Brut y Tywysogyon, or the Chronicle of the Princes: Red Book of Hergest version, ed. T. Jones (Cardiff, 1955).

Calendar of Ancient Correspondence Concerning Wales, ed. J. G. Edwards (Cardiff, 1935).

Calendar of Charter Rolls, vol. 3 (London, 1908).

Calendar of Inquisitions Miscellaneous, 1219–1307 (London, 1916).

Calendar of Inquisitions Post Mortem, vol. 1, *Henry III* (London, 1904); vol. 5, *Edward II* (London, 1908); vol. 7, *Edward III* (London, 1909).

Calendar of Patent Rolls, 1281–92 (London, 1893).

Cartae et alia munimenta quae ad dominium de Glamorgancia pertinent, ed. G. T. Clark, 2nd edn (6 vols, Cardiff, 1910).

The Charters of the Abbey of Ystrad Marchell, ed. G. C. G. Thomas (Aberystwyth, 1997).

'The charters of the boroughs of Brecon and Llandovery', ed. W. Rees, *Bulletin of the Board of Celtic Studies*, 2 (1923–4), 243–61.

The Chronicle of John, Prior of Hexham, in *The Priory of Hexham, its Chroniclers, Endowments and Annals*, ed. J. Raine (2 vols, Durham, 1868), i, 107–72.

Die Chronik des Bischofs Thietmar von Merseburg und ihre Korveier Überarbeitung, ed. R. Holtzmann, in *Monumenta Germaniae Historica, Scriptores rerum Germanicarum*, NS, vol. 9 (Berlin, 1935)

Curia Regis Rolls, vol. 15, *1233–37* (London, 1972).

The Deeds of the Normans in Ireland. La Geste des Engleis en Yrlande, ed. E. Mulally (Dublin, 2002).

Domesday Book, gen. ed. J. Morris, Phillimore edn (Chichester, 1978–); Alecto edn, print and digital, with maps (London, 1987–); The National Archives website's Domesday Book pages are to be found at: *http://www.national archives.gov.uk/domesday/*

'An early charter of the abbey of Cwmhir', ed. B. G. Charles, *The Transactions of the Radnorshire Society*, 40 (1970), 68–73.

The Ecclesiastical History of Orderic Vitalis, ed. and trans. M. Chibnall (6 vols, Oxford, 1969–80).
English Historical Documents, vol. 1, *c.500–1042*, ed. D. Whitelock, 2nd edn (London, 1979).
English Historical Documents, vol. 2, *1042–1189*, ed. D. C. Douglas and G. W. Greenaway (London, 1981).
English Historical Documents, vol. 3, *1189–1327*, ed. H. Rothwell (London and New York, 1975, repr. 2002).
Episcopal Acts and Cognate Documents Relating to Welsh Dioceses, 1066–1272, ed. J. C. Davies (2 vols, Cardiff, 1946–8).
Foreign Accounts of Henry III, 1219–34, ed. F. Cazel (PRS, 44, 1974–5).
Fouke le Fitz Waryn, ed. E. Hathaway, P. T. Ricketts, C. A. Robson and A. D. Wilshere (Oxford, 1975).
George Owen of Henllys, *The Description of Pembrokeshire*, ed. D. Miles (Llandysul, 1994).
Gerald of Wales, *Expugnatio Hibernica: The Conquest of Ireland*, ed. and trans. A. B. Scott and F. X. Martin (Dublin, 1978).
——, *The History and Topography of Ireland*, trans. L. Thorpe (1951, rev. edn. 1982).
——, *The Journey through Wales/The Description of Wales*, trans. L. Thorpe (London, 1978).
Gesta regis Henrici Secundi, ed. W. Stubbs (2 vols, RS, 1867).
Giraldi Cambrensis opera, ed. J. S. Brewer, J. F. Dimock and G. F. Warner (8 vols, RS, 1861–91).
Giraldus Cambrensis, De invectionibus, ed. W. S. Davies in *Y Cymmrodor*, 30 (1920).
Giraldus Cambrensis, Speculum duorum: or, a Mirror of Two Men, ed. Y. Lefèvre and R. B. C. Huygen, trans. B. Dawson, gen. ed. M. Richter (Cardiff, 1974).
Helmold von Bosau, *Helmolds Slavenchronik*, ed. B. Schmeidler, in *Monumenta Germaniae Historica, Scriptores rerum Germanicum in usum scholarum separatim editi*, 32 (Hanover, 1937).
Historia Gruffud vab Kenan, ed. D. Simon Evans (Cardiff, 1977).
The History of Gruffudd ap Cynan, ed. and trans. A. Jones (Manchester, 1910).
History of William Marshal, ed. A. J. Holden, trans. S. Gregory, historical notes by D. Crouch (3 vols, Anglo-Norman Text Society Occasional Publications, 4–6, London, 2002–6).
Innocentii III, Romani pontificis, opera omnia, ed. J.–P. Migne (4 vols, Bibliotheca Patrum Latina, 214–18, Paris, 1855).
Irish Historical Documents, ed. E. Curtis and R. B. McDowell (London, 1943).
'The Irish Pipe Roll of 14 John, 1211–12', ed. O. Davies and D. B. Quinn, in *Ulster Journal of Archaeology*, 3rd series, supplement to vol. 4 (1941).
List of Welsh Entries in the Memoranda Rolls, 1282–1343, ed. N. Fryde (Cardiff, 1974).

Littere Wallie, ed. J. G. Edwards (Cardiff, 1940).
Matthew Paris, *Chronica majora*, ed. H. R. Luard (7 vols, RS, 1872–83).
'Mawl Hywel ap Goronwy', ed. R. Geraint Gruffydd, in *Gwaith Meilyr Brydydd a'i Ddysgynyddion*, ed. J. E. Caerwyn Williams and P. I. Lynch (Cardiff, 1994), no. 10.
A Mediaeval Prince of Wales: The Life of Gruffudd ap Cynan, ed. and trans. D. Simon Evans (Felinfach: Llanerch, 1990).
Monasticon Anglicanum. A History of the Abbies and other Monasteries, Hospitals, Friaries, and Cathedral and Collegiate Churches, with their Dependencies, in England and Wales, ed. W. Dugdale, new edn by J. Caley, H. Ellis and B. Bandinel (6 vols in 8, London, 1817–30; repr. Farnborough, 1970).
The Parliament Rolls of Medieval England, 1275–1504, gen. ed. C. Given-Wilson (16 vols, London, 2005), vol. 1, *1275–94*, ed. P. Brand (London, 2005).
Pipe Roll 31 Henry I, ed. J. Hunter (1833, repr. in facs. London, 1929).
Pipe Roll 25 Henry II, 1178–9 (PRS, 28).
Placita de quo warranto, ed. W. Illingworth (London, 1818).
Ralph of Diss, *Opera historica*, ed. W. Stubbs (2 vols, RS, 1876).
Regesta regum Anglo-Normannorum. The Acta of William I (1066–1087), ed. D. Bates (Oxford, 1998).
The Register of Thomas de Cantilupe, Bishop of Hereford (AD. 1275–1282), ed. R. G. Griffiths and W. W. Capes (Hereford, 1906).
Richard fitz Nigel, *Dialogus de scaccario*, ed. C. Johnson et al., rev. edn (Oxford, 1983).
Roger of Wendover, *Chronica, sive flores historiarum*, ed. H. O. Coxe (4 vols, London, 1841–4).
Rolls of Arms, Henry III, ed. T. D. Tremlett (London, 1967).
Rotuli de oblatis et finibus, tempore regis Johannis, ed. T. D. Hardy (London, 1835).
Saxo Grammaticus, *Saxonis gesta Danorum*, ed. J. Olrik and H. Ræder (2 vols, Copenhagen, 1931–57).
Select Bills in Eyre, 1292–1333, ed. W. C. Bolland (Selden Society 30, 1914).
The Song of Dermot and the Earl. An Old French poem, ed. and trans. G. H. Orpen (Oxford, 1892; repr. Felinfach: Llanerch Press, 1994).
A Survey of the Duchy of Lancaster Lordships in Wales, 1609–13, ed. W. Rees (Cardiff, 1953).
Taxatio ecclesiastica Angliae et Walliae auctoritate P. Nicholai IV. circa A. D. 1291, ed. T. Astle, S. Ayscough, and J. Caley (London, 1802).
Thietmar von Merseburg, *Chronik*, ed. and trans. W. Trillmich (Freiherr vom Stein-Gedächtnisausgabe, 9, Berlin, 1960).
Urkunden und erzählende Quellen zur deutschen Ostsiedlung im Mittelalter, ed. H. Helbig and L. Weinrich (Darmstadt, 1968).
Vincenti Pragensis annales, ed. W. Wattenbach, in *Monumenta Germaniae Historica, Scriptores*, 17 (Hanover, 1861), 658–83.

Vita Griffini filii Conani: The Medieval Latin Life of Gruffudd ap Cynan, ed. and trans. P. Russell (Cardiff, 2005).
Vita Hludowici imperatoris, ed. G. H. Pertz, in *Monumenta Germaniae Historica, Scriptores*, 2 (Hanover, 1829), 604–48.
William of Malmesbury, *Gesta regum*, vol. 1, ed. and trans. R. A. B. Mynors, compl. R. M. Thomson and M. Winterbottom (Oxford, 1998).
William of Newburgh, 'Historia rerum anglicarum', *Chronicles of the Reigns of Stephen, Henry II and Richard I*, ed. R. Howlett (4 vols, RS, 1884–9).

Unpublished Theses

Davies, R. R., 'The Bohun and Lancaster lordships in Wales in the fourteenth and early fifteenth centuries' (University of Oxford D.Phil., 1965).
Evans, B. P., 'The family of Mortimer' (University of Wales Ph.D., 1934).
Holden, B. W., 'The aristocracy of western Herefordshire and the Middle March, 1166–1246' (University of Oxford D.Phil., 2000).
Korngiebel, D., 'English colonization strategies in Ireland and Wales in the thirteenth and fourteenth centuries' (University of Oxford D.Phil., 2005).
Lewis, C. P., 'English and Norman government and lordship in the Welsh borders, 1039–1087' (University of Oxford D.Phil., 1985).
Lieberman, M., 'Shropshire and the March of Wales: the creation of separate identities, *c*.1070–1283' (University of Oxford D.Phil., 2004).
Smith, Ll. B., 'The lordships of Chirk and Oswestry, 1282–1415' (University of London Ph.D., 1971).

Secondary Literature

Aldhouse-Green, M. and R. Howell (eds), *The Gwent County History, vol. 1, Gwent in Prehistory and Early History* (Cardiff, 2004).
Altschul, M., *A Baronial Family in Medieval England: the Clares, 1217–1314* (Baltimore, MD, 1965).
Bapty, I., review of D. Hill and M. Worthington, *Offa's Dyke. History and Guide* (Stroud, 2003), in *Studia Celtica*, 38 (2004), 201–2.
Barker, P. A., 'Timber castles on the Welsh Border with special reference to Hen Domen, Montgomery', in *Les mondes Normands (viiie–xiie siècles)* (Caen, 1989), pp. 135–47.
——, and J. Lawson, 'A pre-Norman field system at Hen Domen, Montgomery', *Medieval Archaeology*, 15 (1972 for 1971), 58–72.
Barrow, G. W. S., *Feudal Britain: The Completion of the Medieval Kingdoms, 1066–1314* (London, 1956).
——, 'The pattern of lordship and feudal settlement in Cumbria', *Journal of Medieval History*, 1 (1975), 130–2.

——, *The Anglo-Norman Era in Scottish History* (Oxford, 1980).
Barrow, J., 'Chester's earliest regatta? Edgar's Dee-rowing revisited', *Early Medieval Europe*, 10 (2001), 81–93.
Bartlett, R., 'Colonial aristocracies of the high Middle Ages', in R. Bartlett and A. MacKay (eds), *Medieval Frontier Societies* (Oxford, 1989), pp. 23–47.
——, *The Making of Europe: Conquest, Colonization and Cultural Change 950–1350* (London, 1993).
——, and A. MacKay (eds), *Medieval Frontier Societies* (Oxford, 1989).
Bateson, M., 'The laws of Breteuil', *English Historical Review*, 15 (1900), 73–8, 302–18, 496–523, 754–7; 16 (1901), 92–110, 332–45.
Bauduin, P., *La première Normandie (x^e–xie siècles): Sur les frontières de la haute Normandie. Identité et construction d'une principauté* (Caen, 2004).
Beresford, M. W., *New Towns of the Middle Ages* (London and New York, 1967).
Boutruche, R., 'The devastation of rural areas during the Hundred Years War and the agricultural recovery of France', in P. S. Lewis (ed.), *The Recovery of France in the Fifteenth Century* (New York and London, 1971), pp. 23–59.
Brand, P., 'Ireland and the literature of the early common law', *Irish Jurist*, NS, 16/1 (1981), 95–113.
Breeze, D. J., *The Northern Frontiers of Roman Britain* (London, 1982).
Broun, D., 'Defining Scotland and the Scots before the Wars of Independence', in D. Broun, R. J. Finlay and M. Lynch (eds), *Image and Identity: The Making and Remaking of Scotland through the Ages* (Edinburgh, 1997), pp. 4–17.
Cam, H. M., 'The evolution of the mediaeval English franchise', *Speculum*, 32 (1957), 427–42; repr. in eadem, *Law-Makers and Law-Finders* (London, 1962), pp. 22–43.
Campbell, J., 'The late Anglo-Saxon state: a maximum view', in idem, *The Anglo-Saxon State* (London, 2000), pp. 1–30.
Carpenter, D. A., *The Struggle for Mastery: Britain 1066–1284* (London, 2003).
Charles, B. G., 'The Welsh, their language and placenames in Archenfield and Oswestry', in *Angles and Britons: O'Donnell Lectures* (Cardiff, 1963), pp. 85–110.
——, *George Owen of Henllys: A Welsh Elizabethan* (Aberystwyth, 1973).
——, *The Place-Names of Pembrokeshire* (Aberystwyth, 1992).
Charles-Edwards, T., *Early Irish and Welsh Kinship* (Oxford, 1993).
——, (ed.), and P. Langford (gen. ed.), *The Short Oxford History of the British Isles: After Rome* (Oxford, 2003).
——, 'The making of nations in Britain and Ireland in the early Middle Ages', in R. Evans (ed.), *Lordship and Learning: Studies in Memory of Trevor Aston* (Woodbridge, 2004), pp. 11–37.

Cosgrove, A. (ed.), *A New History of Ireland*, vol. 2, *Medieval Ireland 1169–1534* (Oxford, 1987).
Coulson, C. L. H., *Castles in Medieval Society* (Oxford, 2003).
Cowley, F. G., *The Monastic Order in South Wales, 1066–1349* (Cardiff, 1977).
Crouch, D., *William Marshal: Court, Career and Chivalry in the Angevin Empire 1147–1219* (London, 1990).
——, *The Image of Aristocracy in Britain, 1000–1300* (London, 1992).
——, 'The March and the Welsh kings', in E. King (ed.), *The Anarchy of King Stephen's Reign* (Oxford, 1994), pp. 256–89.
Davies, J. L., and D. P. Kirby (eds), *Cardiganshire County History*, vol. 1, *From the Earliest Times to the Coming of the Normans* (Cardiff, 1994, repr. 2001).
Davies, J. R., *The Book of Llandaf and the Norman Church in Wales* (Woodbridge, 2003).
——, 'Aspects of Church reform in Wales, $c.1093–c.1223$', *Anglo-Norman Studies*, 30 (forthcoming).
Davies, R. R., 'The survival of the bloodfeud in medieval Wales', *History: The Journal of the Historical Association*, 54 (1969), 338–57.
——, 'The law of the March', *WHR*, 5 (1970), 1–30.
——, *Lordship and Society in the March of Wales, 1282–1400* (Oxford, 1978).
——, 'Kings, lords and liberties in the March of Wales, 1066–1272', *TRHS*, 5th ser., 29 (1979), 41–61.
——, 'Law and national identity in thirteenth-century Wales', in R. R. Davies, R. A. Griffiths, I. G. Jones and K. O. Morgan (eds), *Welsh Society and Nationhood: Historical Essays Presented to Glanmor Williams* (Cardiff, 1984), pp. 51–69.
——, 'Henry I and Wales', in H. Mayr-Harting and R. I. Moore (eds), *Studies in Medieval History Presented to R. H. C. Davis* (London, 1985).
——, (ed.), *The British Isles, 1100–1500: Comparisons, Contrasts and Connections* (Edinburgh, 1988).
——, 'Frontier arrangements in fragmented societies: Ireland and Wales', in R. Bartlett and A. MacKay (eds), *Medieval Frontier Societies* (Oxford, 1989), pp. 77–100.
——, *Domination and Conquest: The Experience of Ireland, Scotland and Wales 1100–1300* (Cambridge, 1990).
——, 'The English state and the "Celtic" peoples, 1100–1400', *Journal of Historical Sociology*, 6 (1993), 1–14.
——, 'The peoples of Britain and Ireland, 1100–1400. 1. Identities', *TRHS*, 6th ser., 4 (1994), 1–20.
——, 'The peoples of Britain and Ireland, 1100–1400. 2. Names, boundaries and regnal solidarities', *TRHS*, 6th ser., 5 (1995), 1–20.
——, *The Revolt of Owain Glyn Dŵr* (Oxford, 1995).
——, 'The peoples of Britain and Ireland, 1100–1400. 3. Laws and customs', *TRHS*, 6th ser., 6 (1996), 1–23.

——, 'The peoples of Britain and Ireland, 1100–1400: 4. Language and historical mythology', *TRHS*, 6th ser., 7 (1997), 1–24.
——, 'Lloyd, Sir John Edward, 1861–1947', *ODNB*.
——, *The Age of Conquest: Wales 1063–1415* (Oxford, 2000; first published under this title Oxford, 1991; originally published as *Conquest, Coexistence and Change: Wales 1063–1415*, Oxford, 1987).
——, *The First English Empire: Power and Identities in the British Isles 1093–1343* (Oxford, 2000).
——, 'The medieval state: the tyranny of a concept?', *Journal of Historical Sociology*, 16 (2003), 280–99.
——, 'The identity of "Wales" in the thirteenth century', in idem and G. H. Jenkins (eds), *From Medieval to Modern Wales: Historical Essays in Honour of Kenneth O. Morgan and Ralph A. Griffiths* (Cardiff, 2004), pp. 45–63.
Davies, S., *Welsh Military Institutions, 633–1283* (Cardiff, 2004).
Davies, W., *Patterns of Power in Early Wales* (Oxford, 1990).
——, and P. Langford (gen. ed.), *The Short Oxford History of the British Isles: From the Vikings to the Normans* (Oxford, 2003).
Dhondt, J., 'Le titre du marquis à l'époque carolingienne', *Archivum Latinitatis Medii Aevi (Bulletin Du Cange)*, 19 (1948), 407–17.
Down, K., 'Colonial society and economy in the high Middle Ages', in A. Cosgrove (ed.), *New History of Ireland*, vol. 2 (Oxford, 1987), pp. 439–91.
Duffy, S., 'The problem of degeneracy', in J. F. Lydon (ed.), *Law and Disorder in Thirteenth-Century Ireland: The Dublin Parliament of 1297* (Dublin, 1997), pp. 87–106.
Duncan, A. A. M., *Scotland: The Making of the Kingdom* (Edinburgh, 1975; repr. 1996).
——, *The Kingship of the Scots, 842–1292: Succession and Independence* (Edinburgh, 2002).
Dyer, C., *Making a Living in the Middle Ages: The People of Britain 850–1250* (New Haven and London, 2002).
Edwards, J. G., 'The Normans and the Welsh March', *Proceedings of the British Academy*, 42 (1957 for 1956), 155–77.
——, *The Principality of Wales, 1267–1967: A Study in Constitutional History* (Denbigh, 1969).
Eyton, R. W., *Antiquities of Shropshire* (12 vols, London, 1854–60).
Flanagan, M. T., *Irish Society, Anglo-Norman Settlers, Angevin Kingship: Interactions in Ireland in the Late Twelfth Century* (Oxford, 1989).
Foot, S., 'The making of *Angelcynn*: English identity before the Norman Conquest', *TRHS*, 6th ser., 6 (1996), 25–49.
Forsyth, K., 'Origins: Scotland to 1100', in J. Wormald (ed.), *Scotland: A History* (Oxford, 2005), pp. 1–37.
Frame, R., *Colonial Ireland* (Dublin, 1981).

——, '"Les Engleys nées en Irlande": the English political identity in medieval Ireland', *TRHS*, 6th ser., 3 (1993), 83–103.
——, *The Political Development of the British Isles, 1100–1400* (Oxford, 1990; pbk, Oxford, 1995).
Gaydon, A. T. (ed.), *A History of Shropshire*, vol. 8 (Oxford, 1968).
Gillingham, J., '1066 and the introduction of chivalry into England', in G. Garnett and J. Hudson (eds), *Law and Government in Medieval England and Normandy: Essays in Honour of Sir James Holt* (Cambridge, 1994), pp. 31–55.
——, 'Killing and mutilating political enemies in the British Isles from the late twelfth to the early fourteenth century: a comparative study', in B. Smith (ed.), *Britain and Ireland 900–1300: Insular Responses to Medieval European Change* (Cambridge, 1999), pp. 114–34.
——, *The English in the Twelfth Century: Nationalism, National Identity and Political Values* (Woodbridge, 2000).
——, 'Conquering the barbarians: war and chivalry in twelfth-century Britain', *Haskins Society Journal*, 4 (1993 for 1992), 67–84; repr. in idem, *The English in the Twelfth Century*, pp. 41–58 and 209–31.
——, 'Henry II, Richard I and the Lord Rhys', *Peritia*, 10 (1996), 225–36; repr. in idem, *The English in the Twelfth Century*, pp. 59–68.
——, 'The English invasion of Ireland', in B. Bradshaw, A. Hadfield and W. Maley (eds), *Representing Ireland: Literature and the Origins of Conflict* (Cambridge, 1993), pp. 24–42; repr. in Gillingham, *The English in the Twelfth Century*, pp. 145–60.
——, '"Holding to the rules of war (*bellica iura tenentes*)": right conduct before, during, and after battle in north-western Europe in the eleventh century', *Anglo-Norman Studies*, 29 (2007) (R. Allen Brown Memorial Lecture), 2–15.
Glasscock, R. E., 'Land and people, *c*.1300', in A. Cosgrove (ed.), *New History of Ireland*, vol. 2 (Oxford, 1987), pp. 205–39.
Graham, B. J., 'The mottes of the Norman liberty of Meath', in H. Murtagh (ed.), *Irish Midland Studies: Essays in Commemoration of N. W. English* (Athlone, 1980), pp. 39–56.
Grant, A., and K. J. Stringer (eds), *Uniting the Kingdom? The Making of British History* (London, 1995).
Griffiths, M., 'The manor in medieval Glamorgan: the estates of the de Ralegh family in the fourteenth and fifteenth centuries', *BBCS*, 32 (1985), 173–201.
——, 'Native society on the Anglo-Norman frontier: the evidence of the Margam charters', *WHR*, 14 (1989), 179–216.
Griffiths, R. A., 'Carmarthen', in idem (ed.), *Boroughs of Mediaeval Wales* (Cardiff, 1978), pp. 131–63.
——, 'Wales and the marches', in D. M. Palliser (ed.), *The Cambridge Urban History of Britain*, vol. 1 (Cambridge, 2000), pp. 681–714.

——, (ed.), and P. Langford (gen. ed.), *The Short Oxford History of the British Isles: The Fourteenth and Fifteenth Centuries* (Oxford, 2003).
——, 'John de Estratlinges (d.c.1293)', *ODNB*.
——, T. Hopkins and R. Howell (eds), *The Gwent County History, vol. 2, The Age of the Marcher Lords, c.1070–1536* (Cardiff, 2008).
Hallam, H. E., 'The climate of eastern England 1250–1350', *Agricultural History Review*, 32 (1984), 124–32.
——, 'The life of the people', in J. Thirsk (ed.), *The Agrarian History of England and Wales*, vol. 2, *1042–1350* (Cambridge, 1988), pp. 818–53.
Harvey, B. (ed.), and P. Langford (gen. ed.), *The Short Oxford History of the British Isles: The Twelfth and Thirteenth Centuries. 1066–c.1280* (Oxford, 2001).
Herrmann, J. (ed.), *Die Slawen in Deutschland* (Berlin, 1985).
Higham, R., and P. A. Barker, *Hen Domen Montgomery: A Timber Castle on the English–Welsh Border. A Final Report* (Oxford, 2000).
Hill, D., and M. Worthington, *Offa's Dyke: History and Guide* (Stroud, 2003).
Hoffman, R. C., 'Warfare, weather and a rural economy: the duchy of Wroclaw in the mid-fifteenth century', *Viator*, 4 (1973), 273–405.
Hogg, A. H. A., and D. J. C. King, 'Castles in Wales and the marches: additions and corrections', *Arch. Camb.*, 119 (1970), 119–24.
——, and ——, 'Early castles in Wales and the marches', *Arch. Camb.*, 112 (1963), 77–124.
——, and ——, 'Masonry castles in Wales and the marches: a list', *Arch. Camb.*, 116 (1967), 71–132.
Holt, J. C., *The Northerners: A Study in the Reign of King John* (Oxford, 1961).
——, *Magna Carta*, 2nd edn (Cambridge, 1992).
Jones, J. G., and E. M. White (eds), *Cardiganshire County History*, vol. 2, *Medieval and Early Modern Cardiganshire* (forthcoming).
Kapelle, W. E., *The Norman Conquest of the North: The Region and its Transformation, 1000–1135* (London, 1979).
King, D. J. C., 'The castles of Ceredigion', *Ceredigion*, 3/1 (1956), 50–69.
——, 'Pembroke castle', *Arch. Camb.*, 127 (1979 for 1978), 75–121.
——, and J. C. Perks, 'Manorbier castle, Pembrokeshire', *Arch. Camb.*, 119 (1970), 83–118.
Latimer, P., 'Henry II's campaign against the Welsh in 1165', *WHR*, 14 (1988), 523–52.
Lewis, C. P., 'An introduction to the Herefordshire Domesday', in A. Williams and R. W. H. Erskine (eds), *The Herefordshire Domesday* (Alecto County Edition of Domesday Book, 6, London, 1988), pp. 1–22.
——, 'The early earls of Norman England', *Anglo-Norman Studies*, 13 (1990), 207–23.
——, 'An introduction to the Cheshire Domesday', in A. Williams and R.W. H. Erskine (eds), *The Cheshire Domesday* (Alecto County Edition of Domesday Book, 20, London, 1991), pp. 1–25.

Lieberman, M., 'Anglicization in high medieval Wales: the case of Glamorgan', *WHR*, 23 (2006), 1–26.

———, 'The English and the Welsh in *Fouke le Fitz Waryn*', *Thirteenth-Century England*, 12 (Woodbridge, forthcoming).

———, *The Medieval Concept of the March of Wales* (Cambridge, forthcoming).

———, 'Striving for Marcher liberties: the Corbets of Caus in the thirteenth century', in M. Prestwich (ed.), *Liberties and Identities in Later Medieval Britain* (Woodbridge, forthcoming).

Lindesay, W., *The Great Wall* (Oxford, 2003).

Lloyd, J. E., *A History of Wales from the Earliest Times to the Edwardian Conquest* (London, 1911; 3rd edn 1939).

Lydon, J. F., 'The middle nation', in idem (ed.), *The English in Medieval Ireland* (Dublin, 1984), pp. 1–26.

McNeill, P. G. B., H. L. MacQueen, and A. M. Lyons (eds), *Atlas of Scottish History to 1707* (Edinburgh, 1996).

MacQueen, H., 'Scots law under Alexander III', in N. H. Reid (ed.), *Scotland in the Reign of Alexander III, 1249–1286* (Edinburgh, 1990), pp. 74–102.

Martin, F. X., 'John, lord of Ireland, 1185–1216', in A. Cosgrove (ed.), *New History of Ireland*, vol. 2 (Oxford, 1987), pp. 127–55.

Mason, J. F. A., 'Roger de Montgomery and his sons (1067–1102)', *TRHS*, 5th ser., 13 (1963), 1–28.

Miller, E. (ed.), *The Agrarian History of England and Wales*, vol. 3, *1348–1500* (Cambridge, 1991).

Nelson, L. H., *The Normans in South Wales, 1070–1171* (Austin, TX, and London, 1966).

O'Byrne, E., and J. Ní Ghradaigh (eds), *The March in the Medieval West, 1000–1400* (forthcoming).

Pierce, G. O., *The Place-Names of Dynas Powys Hundred* (Cardiff, 1968).

———, *Place-Names in Glamorgan* (Cardiff, 2002).

Pohl, W., I. Wood and H. Reimitz (eds), *The Transformation of Frontiers from Late Antiquity to the Carolingians* (Leiden, 2001).

Postles, D., and J. T. Rosenthal (eds), *Studies on the Personal Name in Later Medieval England and Wales* (Kalamazoo, MI, 2006).

Power, D., *The Norman Frontier in the Twelfth and Early Thirteenth Centuries* (Cambridge, 2004).

———, and N. Standen (eds), *Frontiers in Question: Eurasian Borderlands, 700–1700* (London, 1999).

Prestwich, M. (ed.), *Liberties and Identities in Later Medieval Britain* (Woodbridge, forthcoming).

Pryce, H., 'In search of a medieval society: Deheubarth in the writings of Gerald of Wales', *WHR*, 13 (1987), 265–81.

———, 'British or Welsh? National identity in twelfth-century Wales', *English Historical Review*, 116/468 (2001), 775–801.

Pugh, T. B. (ed.), and G. Williams (gen. ed.), *Glamorgan County History*, vol. 3, *The Middle Ages* (Cardiff, 1971).
Quinnell, H., and M. R. Blockley, *Excavations at Rhuddlan, Clwyd, 1969–1973: Mesolithic to Medieval* (York, 1994).
RCAHMW, *An Inventory of the Ancient Monuments in Glamorgan*, vol. 3, part 2, *Medieval Secular Monuments, Non-Defensive* (Cardiff, 1982).
——, *An Inventory of the Ancient Monuments in Glamorgan*, vol. 3, part 1a, *Medieval Secular Monuments: The Early Castles. From the Norman Conquest to 1217* (London, 1991).
——, *An Inventory of the Ancient Monuments in Glamorgan*, vol. 3, part 1b, *Medieval Secular Monuments: The Later Castles. From 1217 to the Present* (Llandudno, 2000).
Reeves, A. C., *The Marcher Lords* (Swansea, 1983).
Robinson, D. M., *The Cistercians in Wales: Architecture and Archaeology 1130–1540* (London, 2006).
Rowlands, I. W., 'The making of the March: aspects of the Norman settlement in Dyfed', *Proceedings of the Battle Conference on Anglo-Norman Studies*, 3 (1981 for 1980), 142–57.
Sanders, I. J., *English Baronies: A Study of their Origin and Descent, 1086–1327* (Oxford, 1960).
Schlesinger, W. (ed.), *Die deutsche Ostsiedlung des Mittelalters als Problem der europäischen Geschichte: Reichenau-Vorträge 1970–1972* (Sigmaringen, 1975).
Schulze, H. K., 'Die Besiedlung der Mark Brandenburg im hohen und späten Mittelalter', *Jahrbuch für die Geschichte Ost- und Mitteldeutschlands*, 28 (1979), 42–178.
Siddons, M. P., *The Development of Welsh Heraldry* (4 vols, Aberystwyth, 1991–2006).
Smith, B. (ed.), *Britain and Ireland 900–1300: Insular Responses to Medieval European Change* (Cambridge, 1999).
Smith, J. B., 'The kingdom of Morgannwg and the Norman conquest of Glamorgan', in T. B. Pugh (ed.) and G. Williams (gen. ed.), *Glamorgan County History*, vol. 3, *The Middle Ages* (Cardiff, 1971), pp. 1–43.
——, 'The middle March in the thirteenth century', *BBCS*, 24 (1970–2), 77–93.
Spurgeon, C. J., 'Builth Castle', *Brycheiniog*, 18 (1978–79), 47–59.
Stenton, F. M., 'The road system of medieval England', *Economic History Review*, 7 (1936), 1–21.
Stephenson, D., 'Madog ap Maredudd: *rex Powissensium*', *WHR* (forthcoming).
Strickland, M., *War and Chivalry: The Conduct and Perception of War in England and Normandy, 1066–1217* (Cambridge, 1996).

Thirsk, J. (ed.), *The Agrarian History of England and Wales*, vol. 2, *1042–1350* (Cambridge, 1988).
Thomas, H. M., *The English and the Normans: Ethnic Hostility, Assimilation, and Identity, 1066–c.1220* (Oxford, 2003).
Thorn, F. R., 'Hundreds and Wapentakes', in A. Williams and R. W. H. Erskine (eds), *The Cheshire Domesday* (Alecto County Edition of Domesday Book, 20, London, 1991), pp. 26–44.
Thornton, D., 'Edgar and the eight kings, AD 973: *textus et dramatis personae*', *Early Medieval Europe*, 10 (2001), 49–79.
Turner, F. J., *The Frontier in American History* (New York, 1921).
Wacher, J. (ed.), *The Roman World* (2 vols, London, 1990).
Walker, D. G., *The Norman Conquerors* (Swansea, 1977).
——, 'Cardiff', in R. A. Griffiths (ed.), *Boroughs of Mediaeval Wales* (Cardiff, 1978), pp. 103–28.
Walker, R. F. (ed.), *Pembrokeshire County History*, vol. 2, *Medieval Pembrokeshire* (Haverfordwest, 2002).
Whittaker, C. R., *Frontiers of the Roman Empire* (Baltimore, MD, 1994).
Williams, A., 'An introduction to the Worcestershire Domesday', in idem and R. W. H. Erskine (eds), *The Worcestershire Domesday* (Alecto County Edition of Domesday Book, 5, London, 1988), pp. 1–31.
Williams, D. H., *The Welsh Cistercians*, vol. 2 (Tenby, 1984).
——, *Atlas of Cistercian Lands in Wales* (Cardiff, 1990).
——, 'The exploration and excavation of Cistercian sites in Wales', *Arch. Camb.*, 144 (1997 for 1995), 1–25.
Williams-Jones, K., *The Merioneth Lay Subsidy Roll, 1292–3* (Cardiff, 1976).
Wormald, P., 'Bede, the *bretwaldas* and the origins of the *gens Anglorum*', in idem, D. Bullough, and R. Collins (eds), *Ideal and Reality in Frankish and Anglo-Saxon Society: Studies Presented to John Michael Wallace-Hadrill* (Oxford, 1983), pp. 99–129.
——, '*Engla lond*: the making of an allegiance', *Journal of Historical Sociology*, 7/1 (1994), 1–24.

Maps

1 The March of Wales in the fourteenth century

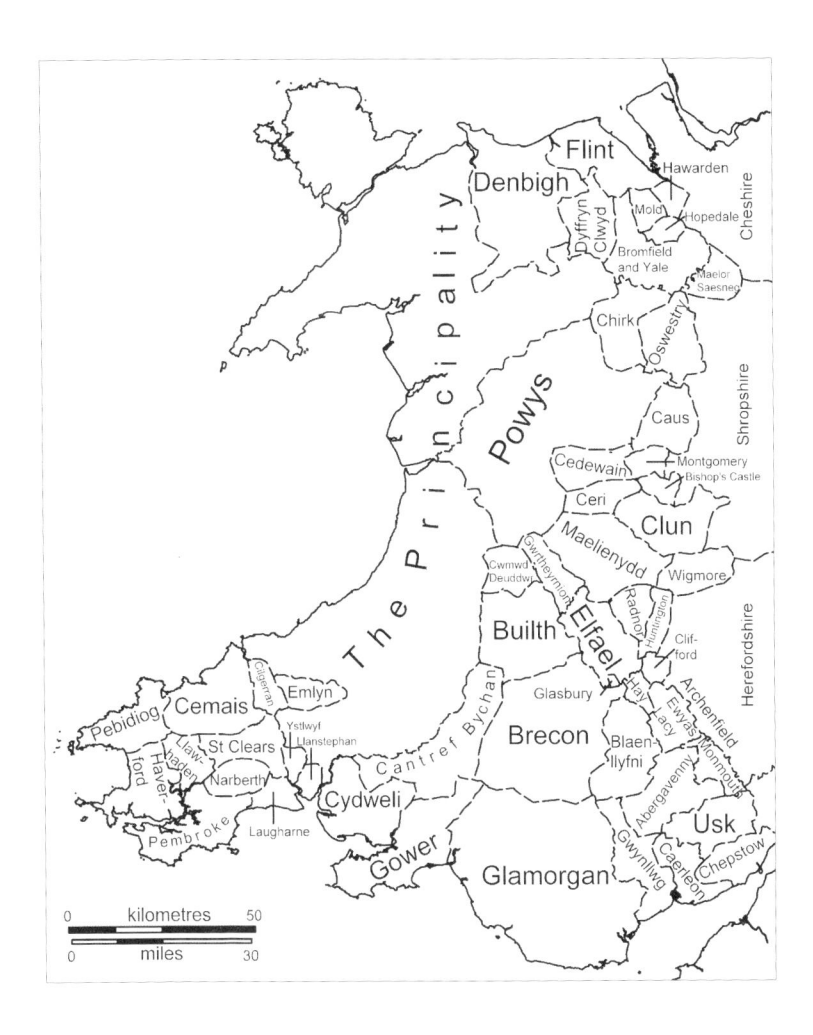

2 Wales and its borders in the eleventh century

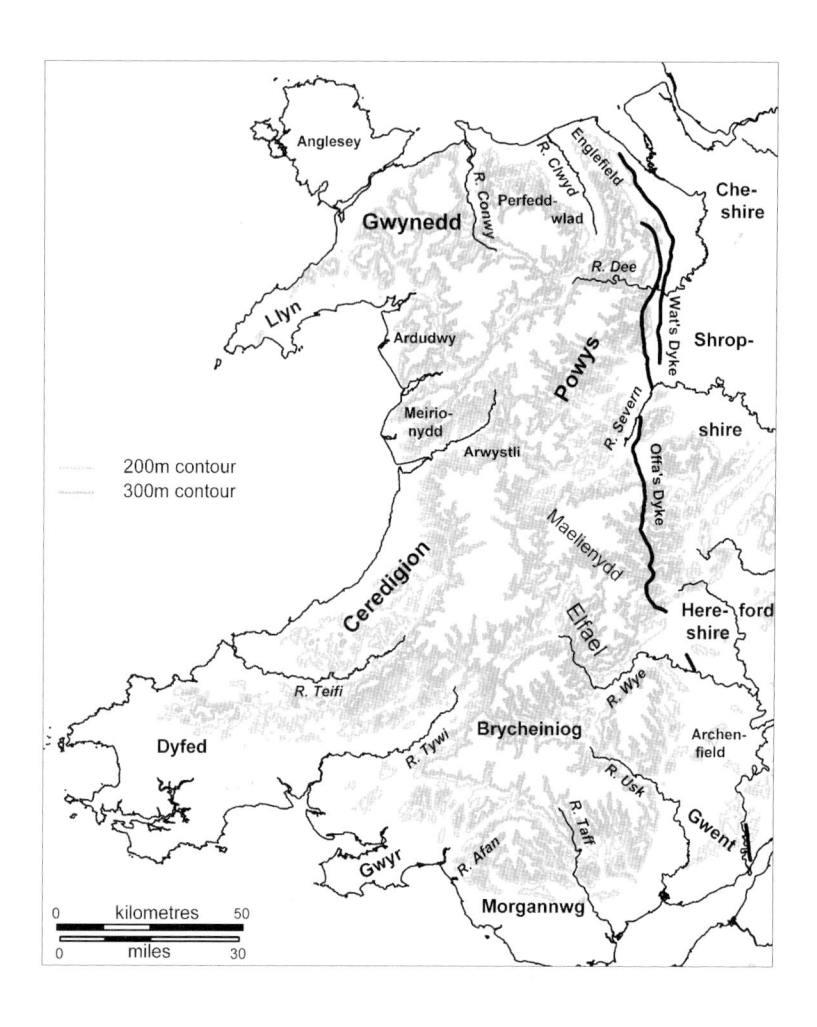

MAPS

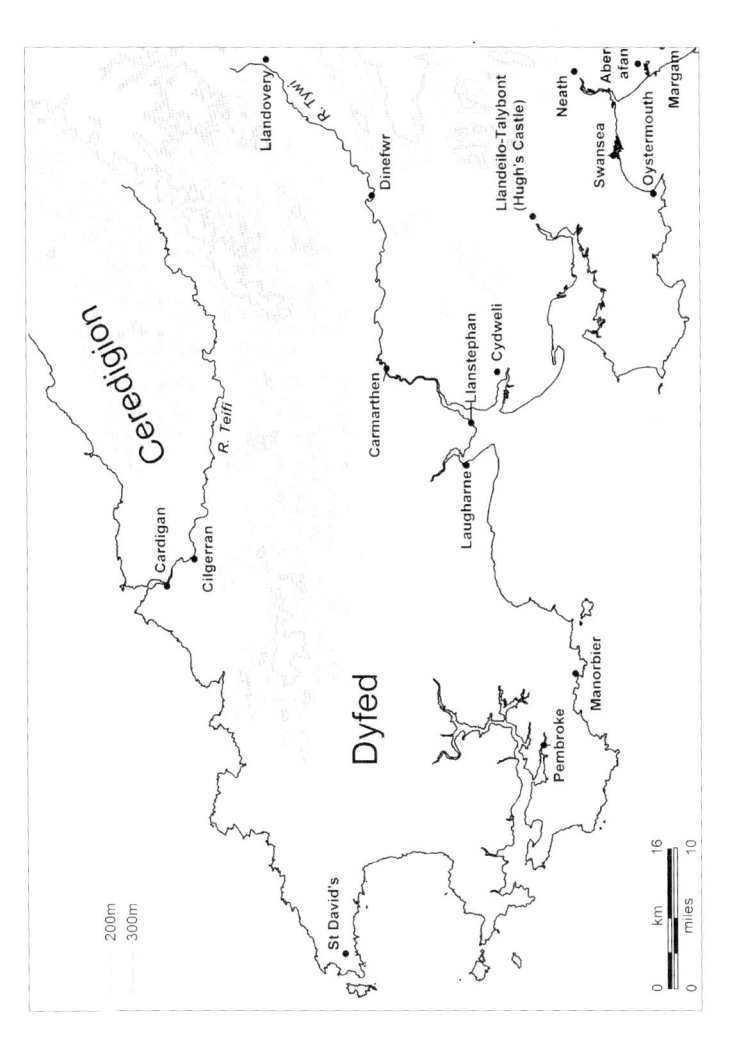

3 The March in the making: the south-west

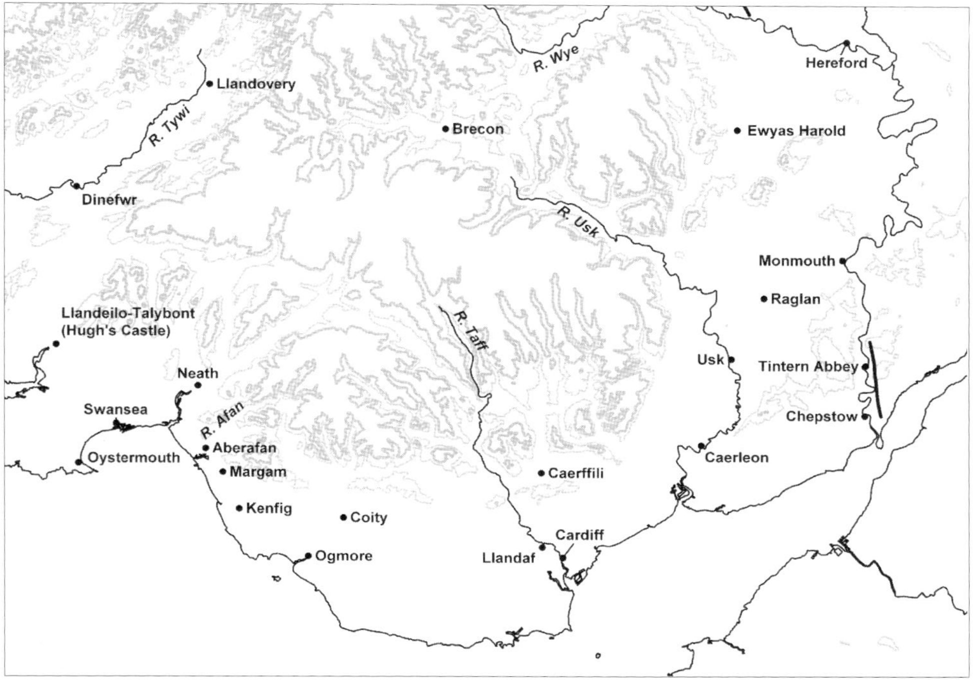

4 The March in the making: the south-east

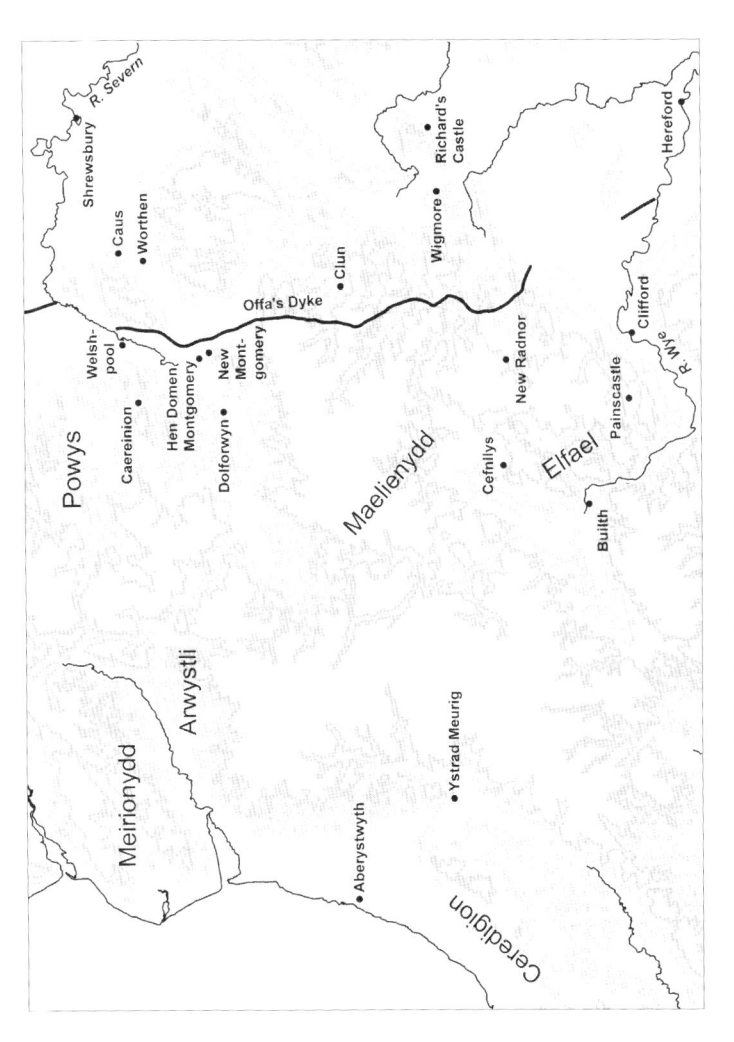

MAPS

5 The March in the making: the middle March

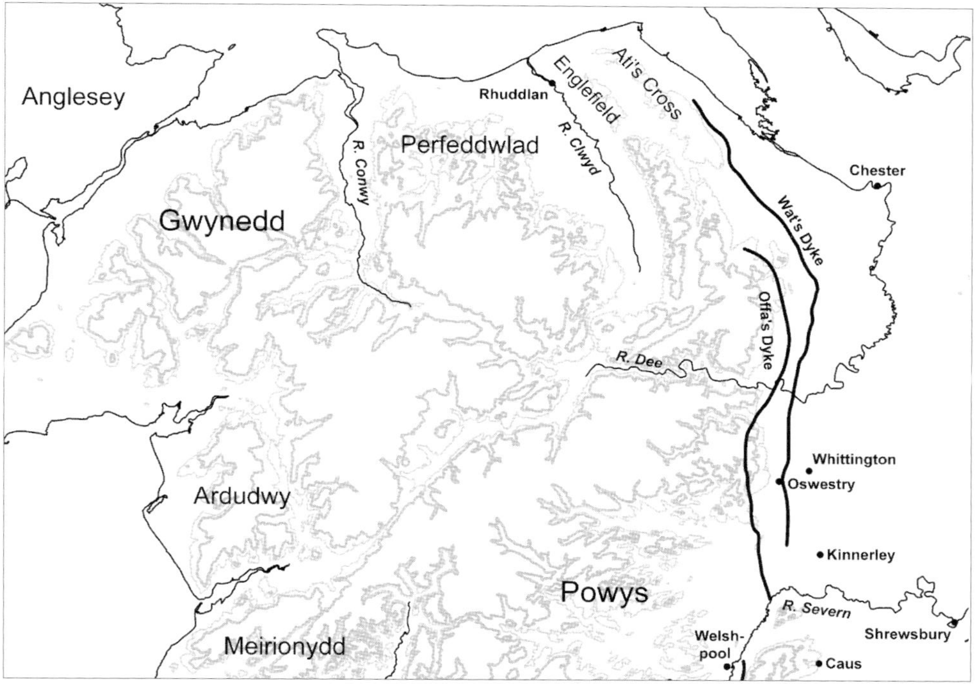

6 The March in the making: the north

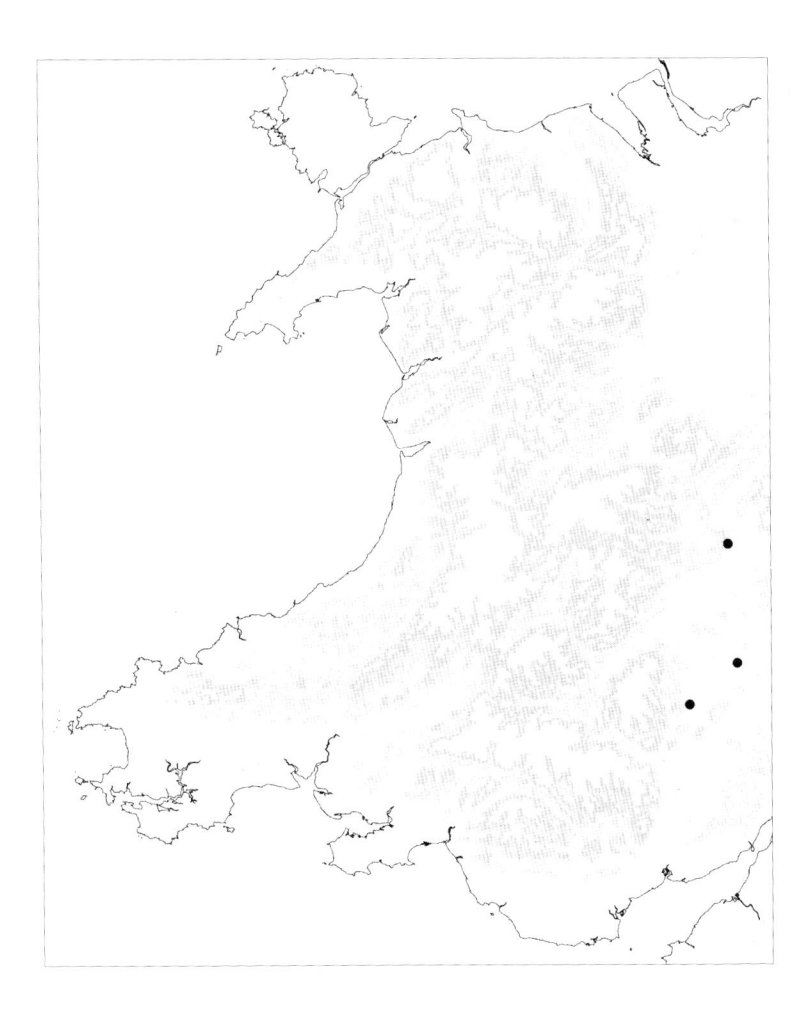

7 Castles in Wales and the borders, 1066

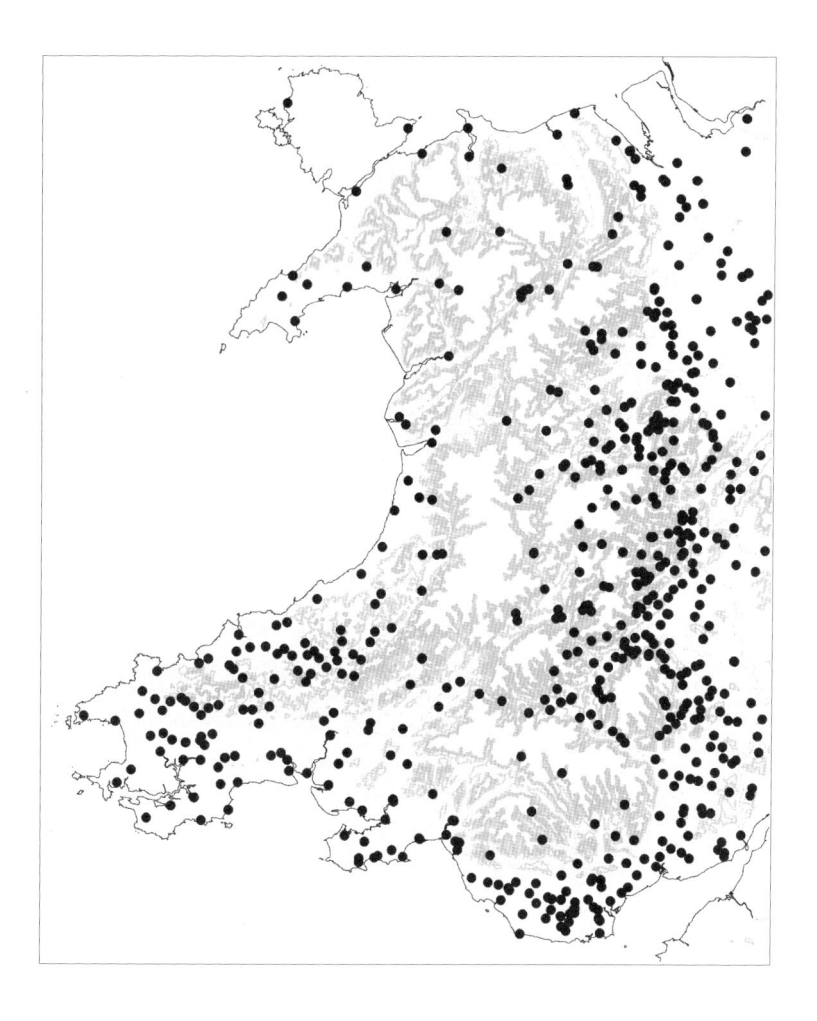

8 Castles in Wales and the March, 1215

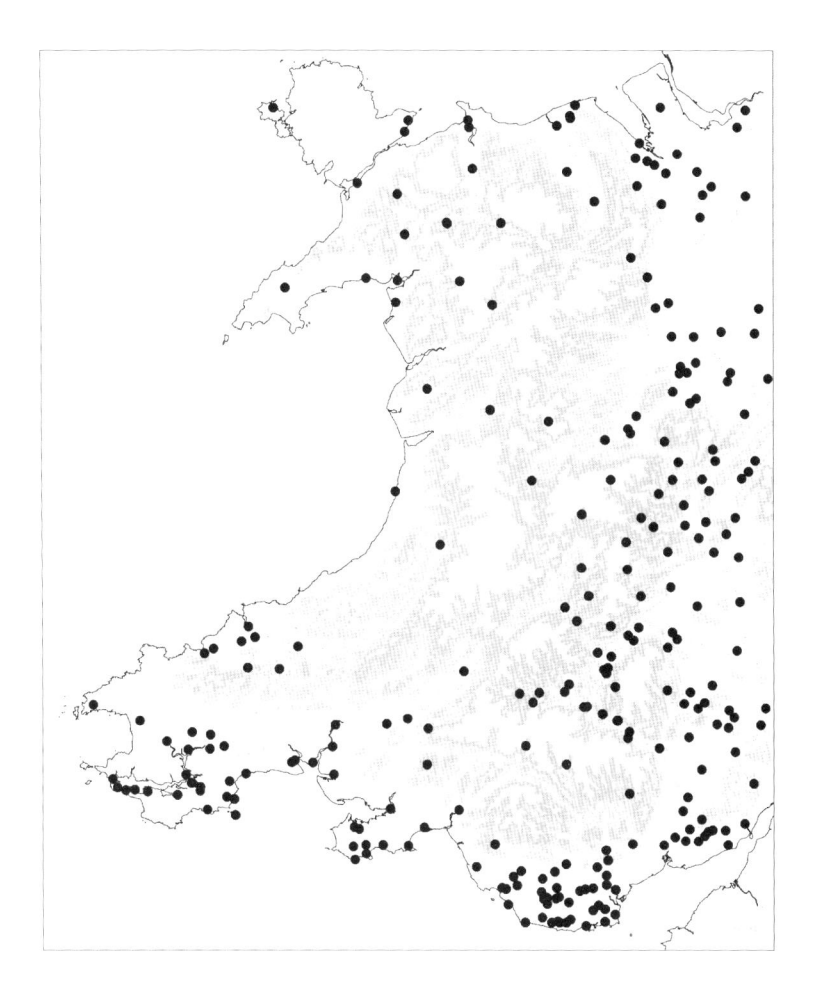

9 Castles in Wales and the March, 1300

Index

Aberafan Welsh borough (maps 3 and 4) 43
Aberystwyth (map 5)
   castles at 24, 34 n. 20, 67, 108
Acts of Union (1536 and 1542) 1, 5, 109
Afan (maps 2, 3 and 4) 60, 68
Albrecht (Albert) the Bear (d.1170) 93–5
Alexander III, king of Scotland (d.1286) 12 n. 7
Anglesey (maps 2 and 6) 1, 22, 46, 71 n. 33, 108
Anglicization 68, 98–9 *see also* English institutions *under* Ireland; March of Wales; Scotland
Archenfield (Erging) (maps 1, 2 and 4) 60–1, 80–2, 86–7, 88
Arnulf de Montgomery (d.1118x22) 16, 22, 56, 82
Arundel, earls of 6, 29, 73 n. 86
Arwystli (maps 2 and 5) 22, 108
Athelstan, king of the English d.939 79, 80

Baderon family 29, 107
   see also John of Monmouth
Barrow, Geoffrey 10–11
Bartlett, Robert 96–8
Beaumont, William de, earl of Warwick and lord of Gower (d.1184) 26, 106
Bernard, first Norman bishop of St David's (d.1148) 58

Bernard de Neufmarché, first Norman lord of Brecon (d.1121x5?) 23, 59
Bernard of Clairvaux (d.1153) 102 n. 24
Bigod family 29
Black Death, the 38, 49
Bohun family 5, 29
Bordeaux, vineyards of 37
boroughs and towns 3, 21, 63, 66, 67
   in Europe generally 37, 93, 94, 95–7, 99
   in Ireland 25, 96
   in the March 43–4, 48–9, 69, 99, 112
   in Wales 43
   see also 'liberties of Breteuil'
Braose family 29, 106, 107
   William I (*fl.* 1090s) 17
   William II (d.1192x3) 26
   William V (d.1230) 17
Brecon (map 4)
   borough 43, 60, 66
   lordship 2, 5, 6, 24, 29, 39–40, 65, 106
   law of 61
Britain
   countries of 75–6
   'British' identity 55–6, 77, 112
   see also Cumbria; England; identities; Scotland; Wales
British Isles
   English empire in 84–5
   'Europeanization' and 'Anglicization' in 98–9
   historiography on 10–11

Builth (map 4)
  castle 16–18, 34 n. 20, 67, 107
  lordship 6, 106, 108
Buttington, battle at (893x4) 19

Cadwallon ap Madog, ruler of Maelienydd (d.1179) 26
Cadwgan ap Bleddyn (d.1111) 24, 59
Caereinion (map 5) 66
Caerffili (map 4) 16, 31, 108
Caerleon (map 4) 26, 29
Cardiff (map 4) 31, 44
  borough 43, 48
  castle 47, 60
  sheriff of Glamorgan and lord at 82, 99
  Welsh food-rent owed at 60
Cardigan castle (map 3) 24, 67, 107
Carmarthen (map 3) 23
  burgages at 43
  castle 30, 107
  'honor' 82–3
castles
  built by Edward I 18, 34 n. 20
  in Wales and the March, survey 15–16
  see also maps 7, 8 and 9 *and individual castles*
Caus (maps 5 and 6) 3, 5, 29, 31, 41, 49, 61
Cefnllys borough (map 5) 48–9
Ceredigion (maps 2, 3 and 5) 1, 13 n. 28
Charlemagne
  his coins 97
  his 'marches' 91
Chepstow (map 4)
  castle 20, 34 n. 31, 105
  lords or lordship 26–9, 50
Cheshire (maps 1, 2 and 6) 5, 30, 79, 80, 107
Chester (map 6) 87
  earls or earldom 21, 22, 105 *see also* Hugh d'Avranches
  justiciars 29
chivalry *see* March of Wales; Wales
Cilgerran castle (map 3) 67, 107

Cistercians *see* March of Wales, monks in; Wales
Clare family 10, 29, 31, 62, 68, 106
  Gilbert (d.1117) 24, 42, 105
    his men in Ceredigion 24, 105
  Gilbert, fifth earl of Gloucester and fourth earl of Hertford (d.1230) 73 n. 86
  Gilbert, 'the Red', seventh earl of Gloucester and sixth earl of Hertford (d.1295) 108
  Gilbert 'Strongbow', earl of Pembroke (d.1148) 17
  Isabel, countess of Pembroke (d.1220)
  Richard (d.1136) 66
  Richard 'Strongbow', earl of Pembroke (d.1176) 28, 35 n. 54
Clifford (map 5) 2, 3, 107
  borough 43
  castle 34 n. 31
Clifford family 29, 107
  Roger, lord of Hawarden 68
  Walter (d.1263) 2, 6
Clun (map 5)
  'hallmoot of the Welsh' 82
  lordship 5, 6, 29, 59, 60
  law of 61
  manor 40
  Welshry 48
Clwyd (maps 1, 2 and 6) 25
Coity (map 4) 4, 48
Corbet family 3, 31
  Peter (d.1300) 3
  Roger (*fl.* 1086) 3, 29, 41
  Thomas (d.1274) 29
crusades 26, 38, 56, 60, 65, 86, 92, 93, 106
Cumberland 4, 12 n. 7, 83
Cumbria 4, 47, 55, 75, 88
  see also Britain, countries of
Cydweli (map 3) 23, 30, 38
  borough 48, 49
  lordship 38, 47

Dafydd ap Gruffudd, prince of Gwynedd (d.1283) 1, 68, 73 n. 82, 108

INDEX

Danelaw, the 20, 45, 78, 87
David I, king of Scotland (d.1153) 64, 99
Davies, Rees 9, 10, 14 n. 34, 76, 83, 111–13
Dee (maps 2 and 6) 19, 25
Despenser family 6
Diarmait MacMurchada, king of Leinster (d.1171) 96
Dinefwr castle (map 3) 67
Dolforwyn castle (map 5) 3
Domesday Book 1, 12 n. 1, 22, 34 n. 31, 40, 78–80, 82, 105
Dyfed (maps 2 and 3) 16, 21, 23, 42, 81, 111
Dyffryn Clwyd (map 1) 2

Eadric 'the Wild' (*fl.* 1067–72) 21
Edgar, king of England (d.975) 19
Edward I, king of England (d.1307) 1–3, 17–18, 28, 31, 33, 34 n. 20, 41, 51, 85, 87, 99, 100, 108–9
  castles in Wales 18, 34 n. 20
Edward II, king of England (d.1327) 1, 6, 109
Edward the Confessor, king of England (d.1066) 18
Edward the Elder, king of Wessex (d.924) 79
Edwards, (John) Goronwy 9
Edwin, earl of Mercia (d.1071) 20
Elfael (maps 1, 2 and 5) 24, 48, 106
Erging *see* Archenfield
England
  'Europeanization' of 98
  kings *see individual kings*
  law 61, 84–5
  as 'state' or 'nation-state'
    before 1066 77–81, 87–8, 98, 113
    thereafter 2, 4, 9, 76, 81–8, 98, 100, 101, 113
  weather 38
  see also Britain, countries of; identities; English institutions *under* Ireland; March of Wales; Scotland; Offa's Dyke
Englefield (maps 2 and 6) 25, 80–2

Ethelred II, king of England (d.1016) 19
'Europeanization of Europe' 96–9, 101, 113
  see also England; Ireland; Poland; Scotland; Wales
Ewyas Harold castle (map 4) 18, 34 n. 31, 105

Falaise (Normandy) 81
fitz Baderon family *see* Baderon family
Fitzalan family 29
  John II (d.1267) 48, 73 n. 86
  Edmund (d.1326) 6
Fitzwarin family 8, 69
  Fulk I (d.1170x71)
  Fulk III (d.1258) 8, 106
frontier studies 7, 11, 76, 89 n. 8, 91

Gerald of Wales 16, 52 n. 18, 112
  family connections 16, 35 n. 54, 57–9, 60, 65
  identity 57–8, 69
  on the English 57, 86
  on Marcher economy 39–40, 47, 100
  on population in Wales and the March 41
  on warfare 64–5, 66, 73 n. 55
  on the Welsh 46, 55, 59, 66, 86, 100
  preaches Third Crusade in Wales 26, 60, 86, 106
Gerald of Windsor (*fl. c.*1100) 16, 57
German-Slavic border 37, 91–5
  Flemings on 92–3
  see also Ostsiedlung
Gloucester, earls of 5, 6, 10, 26, 43, 50, 106
Gloucestershire 5, 43, 79
Gruffudd ap Cynan, king of Gwynedd (d.1137) 24, 106
Gruffudd ap Llywelyn, king of Gwynedd and Deheubarth (d.1063) 18–19, 21, 59, 105
Gruffudd ap Rhys ap Tewdwr (d.1137) 66

Gwynedd (maps 2 and 6) 31, 46
  castles in 66
  rulers of 17–18, 23–5, 30–2, 58–9, 61, 76, 105–6

Harold, king of England (d.1066)
  as Earl Harold 19
  as king 20
Harold the Hard, king of Norway (d.1066) 20
Hen Domen Montgomery castle (map 5) 40
  burgages and 'town' at 48
  field system at 40
Henry I, king of England (d.1135) 23–4, 25, 32, 42, 47, 82–3, 99, 105–6
Henry II, king of England (d.1189) 4, 25–6, 28, 29, 32, 83–4, 95–6, 99, 106
Henry III, king of England (d.1272) 2, 5, 6, 12 n. 7, 17, 30–1, 32, 107–8
  minority government of 30, 36 n. 66
Henry VIII, king of England (d.1547) 5
Henry the Young King (d.1183) 28
Hereford (maps 4 and 5) 79
  bishop 60
  castle 18, 105
  city and cathedral 19
  earls 5, 6, 21, 22 see also William fitz Osbern
  'liberties of Breteuil' at 43
  Offa's Dyke and 77
Herefordshire (maps 1, 2, 4 and 5) 2, 5, 18, 20, 23, 27, 68, 77, 79–80
Hertford, earls 6
Hubert de Burgh, earl of Kent, justiciar (d.1243) 107
Hugh d'Avranches 'the Fat', earl of Chester (d.1101) 21, 22, 81, 105
Hugh de Montgomery (d.1098) 21, 22, 56
Hugh's Castle (Llandeilo-Talybont) (maps 3 and 4) 67
Hundred Years War 37

hundreds see England, as 'state' or 'nation-state'; English institutions under Ireland; March of Wales; Scotland
Hungarians 38

Iberian Peninsula see Spain
identities 11, 112
  English 55–7, 70 nn. 1, 11, 75, 77–8, 101, 112
  English in Ireland 58–9
  Irish 55, 82, 85, 98, 100
  in March of Wales 57–62, 69, 88
  Norman 56, 112
  Scottish 46, 55, 75, 98, 112
  Welsh 55–8, 68–9, 73n. 87, 75, 76–7, 98, 101, 112
  see also Britain; Gerald of Wales
Ireland 5, 10, 17, 25–9, 37, 41–2, 46, 57, 58, 95–100
  English institutions in 83–5, 90 n. 36
  kings see Diarmait MacMurchada; Ruaidrí Ua Conchobair
  see also boroughs and towns; identities
Isabella, queen of England (d.1358) 6

John, king of England (d.1216) 6, 8, 17, 26, 27, 28, 29–30, 32, 83–4, 106–7
John de Courcy (d.1219?) 96
John of Monmouth (d.1248) 17, 29, 107

Kenfig castle (map 4) 82
Kinnerley (map 6) 31

Lacy family 29, 84, 107
  Hugh (d.1186) 84, 95
  Walter (d.1085) 21
Laugharne (map 3) 48
'liberties of Breteuil' 43, 96–7
Llandaf (map 4) 80, 86
Llandovery castle (maps 3 and 4) 67
Llanstephan (map 3) 48
Lloyd, John Edward 8–9, 111, 113
Llŷn (map 1) 21

INDEX

Llywelyn ab Iorwerth, ruler of Gwynedd (d.1240) 17, 28–9, 30, 31, 32, 36 n. 66, 66, 67, 68, 73 n. 70, 74 n. 88, 107
Llywelyn ap Gruffudd, prince of Wales (d.1282) 1, 3, 17–18, 31, 32, 58, 67–8, 73 n. 82, 108

Madog ap Maredudd, king of Powys (d.1160) 24, 106
Maelienydd (maps 1, 2 and 5) 24, 26, 27, 31, 48, 66, 106
Magna Carta 1, 26, 61, 84, 107
Malcolm IV, king of Scotland (d.1165) 4, 83
Manorbier (map 3) 39
March, earl of 6
March of Wales
　assarts in 45 *see also* 95, 97
　chivalry in 63–9, 112–13
　concept 1–2, 12 n. 1, 33
　English institutions in 81–3, 98–9
　Englishries in 48, 86, 100
　field-names in 39, 45–6
　Flemings in 42, 47, 70 n. 7, 82, 86 *see also* 92–3
　historians and 7–11
　interpreters and multilingualism in 60–1
　knights' fees in 5, 44, 62, 69, 99
　law of 61–2
　lordships of *see* map 1 *and individual entries*
　mentioned in sources 1, 26–7, 33
　manors in 31, 40–1, 44–8, 61, 82, 100
　monks in 41, 45, 50, 86, 112 *see also* 93, 95, 96
　origin of word 'march' 12 n. 1
　peasants in 41–2, 43–4, 45–6, 49, 56, 60, 78, 86, 99 *see also* 92–7
　personal names in 43, 45, 59–60, 62, 68, 69, 82 *see also* 97
　place-names in 2, 24, 45–6, 47, 49, 60–1, 86, 112 *see also* 94
　population of 38, 41–2, 43, 51, 87, 99–100 *see also* 95
　socage tenure in 45
　Welshries in 48, 60, 82, 86, 100
　see also boroughs; castles; Gerald of Wales; identities
Marcher liberties 2–4, 59, 85–7
　debate on origins 8–9
Marcher lords *see* Key Dates *and individual families*
　dynasties 29, 106, 107
　entrepreneurship 38–41
　and kings of England 5–6, 23, 26, 27, 31 *see also individual kings*
　legends and romances about 7–8, 68–9
　referred to as *barones Marchie*, 'barons of the March' 27
Margam (maps 3 and 4)
　abbey 45, 50
　'Welsh hundred of the county of' 82
Marshal family 29, 107, 108
　Gilbert, seventh earl (d.1241) 107
　Richard, sixth earl (d.1234) 5, 107
　Walter, eighth earl (d.1245) 107
　William the Marshal, fourth earl of Pembroke (d.1219) 17, 27–8, 41, 73 n. 86
　William Marshal the younger, fifth earl (d.1231) 30, 107
Meirionydd (maps 2, 5 and 6) 3
Mercia 18, 20, 77–9
Monmouth castle (map 4) 2, 20
　abbey 50
　lords or lordship 29, 50, 107
Montgomery (map 5)
　borough 49
　castle (New Montgomery) 2
　earls of Shrewsbury *see* Hugh de Montgomery; Robert de Bellême; Roger de Montgomery
　lordship 3, 86, 107
　Treaty of 17, 108
Morcar, earl of Northumbria (*fl.* 1065–87) 20
Mortimer family 8, 27, 29, 31, 38–9, 49, 58
　Edmund I (d.1304) 87
　Hugh III (d.1227) 27–8

Ralph I (*fl. c.*1080–1104)
Roger II (d.1214) 26, 30, 66, 106
Roger III (d.1282) 3, 31, 58, 67–8, 73 n. 86, 108
Roger V, first earl of March (d.1330) 6
Muslims 38, 91

Neath (maps 3 and 4) 50, 53 n. 58
Nest (d. *c.*1130), daughter of Rhys ap Tewdwr 57
Nest/Agnes, daughter of the Herefordshire lord Osbern fitz Richard, granddaughter of Gruffudd ap Llywelyn 59
New Radnor (map 5)
  borough 48
  castle 106
Northampton, earls of 5
Northumberland 4, 12 n. 7
Northumbria 20, 47

Offa, king of Mercia (d.796) 78
Offa's Dyke (maps 2, 4, 5 and 6) 3, 19–20, 40, 76–80, 86, 87, 113
Ogmore (map 4) 4, 48
Orderic Vitalis (d. *c.*1142) 65, 79
Ostsiedlung 93
  see also German-Slavic border
Oswestry (maps 1 and 6) 6, 24–5, 29, 106
Owain Cyfeiliog (d.1197) 69
Owain Glyn Dŵr (d. *c.*1416) 6, 101
Owain Gwynedd, king of Gwynedd (d.1170) 25, 106
Owen, George, of Henllys (d.1613) 8, 111
Oystermouth (maps 3 and 4)

Painscastle (map 5) 107
  borough 48
Pembroke (map 3)
  castle 16–17, 18, 22, 23, 39, 56, 57, 82
  earls, earldom or county 5, 10, 17, 26, 27, 28, 29, 35 n. 54, 82–3, 99, 106, 107
Peter's Pence 41, 52 n. 18

pleas of the crown 2–4
Poland 37, 91–3, 95, 97
Powys, Welsh dynasty of 24, 31, 59, 61, 65, 69, 106
Principality of Wales 1, 3, 12 n. 2, 31, 76, 84, 108

Raglan castle (map 4) 20
Rhuddlan (map 6) 19, 34 n. 20, 80, 108
Rhys ap Gruffudd, ruler of Deheubarth, the Lord Rhys (d.1197) 17, 26, 30, 66, 106
Rhys ap Tewdwr, ruler of Deheubarth (d.1093) 22, 71 n. 17, 81, 105
Rhys Ieuanc (d.1222) 67
Richard I, king of England (d.1199) 26, 28, 29, 106
Richard's Castle (map 5) 18, 105
Robert de Bellême, earl of Shrewsbury (d.1130 or after) 22, 105
Robert de Tilleul ('of Rhuddlan') *see* Robert of Rhuddlan
Robert fitz Hamo (d.1107) 23, 81–2
Robert of Rhuddlan (d.1088) 21, 22, 65
Roger de Montgomery, earl of Shrewsbury (d.1094) 3, 16, 21, 29, 34 n. 32, 40, 56, 81, 105
royal seal, messenger forced to swallow 2
Ruaidrí Ua Conchobair (Rory O'Connor), high-king of Ireland (d.1198) 42

St David 59
St David's (map 3) 22, 58
St Eluned 39
Saracens *see* Muslims
Scotland 10, 25, 29, 59, 63, 64, 75, 79
  'Anglicization' and 'Europeanization' of 98–9
  border 4, 98
  concept 75
  English institutions in 99
  kings 19, 25, 64, 99 *see also individual kings*

INDEX

Normans in 59
see also Britain, countries of;
identities
Senghennydd 31, 108
Severn (maps 2, 5 and 6) 3, 18, 19, 21, 40, 46, 62, 67, 77
sheriffs 2, 3, 99 *see also* shires
shires *see* England as 'state' or 'nation-state'; English institutions *under* Ireland; March of Wales; Scotland
Shrewsbury (maps 5 and 6) 3, 28, 30, 49, 107
  earls or earldom 3, 16, 21, 22, 29, 40, 56, 105
Shropshire (maps 1, 2, 5 and 6) 3, 5, 6, 21, 25, 30, 31, 68, 77, 79, 86, 87, 105
Slavic-German border *see* German-Slavic border
Slavic gods 92, 94
Snowdonia (Gwynedd) (maps 2 and 6) 1
Spain/Iberian Peninsula 38, 91
Statute of Rhuddlan (1284) 3, 33, 84, 108
Stephen, king of England (d.1154) 6, 17, 23–4, 25, 32, 45, 106
Strathclyde *see* Cumbria
Strättlingen in modern-day Switzerland 100
Strigoil *see* Chepstow
Swansea (maps 3 and 4)
  borough and burgesses 43, 49
  castle 60
  earliest charter 54 n. 65

Tegeingl *see* Englefield
Tintern abbey (map 4) 50
Tudor family 6 *see also* Henry VIII
Tynedale, 'liberty' 4, 12 n. 7

Usk (map 4)
  castle 20
  lordship 26, 29, 62

Valence family 29
Vikings 19, 20, 22, 38, 64, 96, 105

Vincent of Prague 93

Wales
  bloodfeud in 65
  chivalry in 74 n. 88
  Cistercians in 41, 50, 112
  concept 9, 33, 55, 75–7, 99
  economy 46–7
  'Europeanization' and 'Anglicization' of 98
  kingdoms, commotes and *cantrefs* in 2–4 *see also* map 2 *and individual entries*
  law 61–2, 65, 77
  Normans in 18–24, 59
  political fragmentation 75
  population 41–2
  rulers *see* Key Dates *and individual entries*
  as source of territories for English kings to grant their followers 24, 32
  see also boroughs and towns; Britain, countries of; castles; Gerald of Wales; identities; March of Wales; Offa's Dyke
warfare
  and chivalry *see* March of Wales; Wales
  economic effects of 37
  see also Gerald of Wales
Warin 'the bald' (d. *c*.1085) 21
Wat's Dyke (maps 2 and 6) 80
Welshpool (maps 5 and 6) 67, 68
Wessex 27, 79, 105
Westmorland 4, 12 n. 7, 83–4
Whittington (maps 1 and 6) 8, 69, 106, 108
Wigmore (map 5)
  borough 43
  castle 20, 27, 28, 29, 34 n. 31, 105
  lords or lordship 3, 8, 26, 27, 29, 31, 38, 66, 73 n. 86, 87, 106, 108
  priory, chronicle of 38–9
William, earl of Gloucester (d.1183) 26, 81
William I, king of England (d.1087) 8, 20, 21, 22, 23, 32, 56, 63, 105

William II, king of England (d.1100) 23, 32, 70 n. 11, 105
William fitz Osbern (d.1071) 20–1, 22, 28, 34 n. 31, 43, 105
   his son, Roger de Breteuil (*fl.* 1071–87) 22

Wye (maps 2, 4 and 5) 79–80
Worthen (map 5) 41

Ystrad Meurig (map 5)
   castle at 24